# The Seashore Naturalist's Handbook

Published 1981 by
The Hamlyn Publishing Group Limited
London · New York · Sydney · Toronto
Astronaut House, Feltham, Middlesex, England.

© Copyright The Hamlyn Publishing Group Limited 1981

ISBN 0 600 36447 X

Printed in Italy

# The Seashore Naturalist's Handbook

## Leslie Jackman

**Hamlyn**

London · New York · Sydney · Toronto

*Previous page:*
The shells of a spiny cockle. They are
sometimes washed ashore by storms.

This book is concerned with the more common plants and animals that you may find
on the seashores in Britain and Europe. This area has several different marine
regions and conditions, and some species are therefore only found in certain areas.
The identification sections include more species than could be covered in the text.
They are not drawn to scale, but the approximate size of each is given.

# Acknowledgements

*Photographs*
Heather Angel, Farnham 2–3, 15 bottom, 17, 25, 28 bottom, 45, 63 bottom,
67 inset, 70, 79, 84–85, 90–91, 97, 115 left, 146, 149, 150, 159, 164, 166–167,
178 top; Ardea, London – Ian Beames 125; Ardea – Ken Hoy 94; Ardea – Peter
Lamb 99 right; Ardea – P. Morris 155; Ardea – R.F. Porter 115 right; S.C.
Bisserot, Bournemouth 144–145; Bruce Coleman, Uxbridge – Jane Burton front
jacket inset bottom right, 64, 95 top, 156, 158; Bruce Coleman – Robert Burton
12–13; Bruce Coleman – Udo Hirsch – 99 left, 178 bottom; Bruce Coleman –
Gordon Langsbury 101; Bruce Coleman – Derek Middleton 169; Bruce Coleman
– Michael W. Richards/RSPB 87; Bruce Coleman – Dr Frieder Sauer 63 top;
W.F. Davidson, Penrith 108–109, back jacket; Ecology Pictures, Dunblane –
Susan Proctor front jacket, 86; Brian Hawkes, Sittingbourne 111, 118–119, 128,
152–153; Eric Hosking, London 162–163, 174–175, 181; Leslie Jackman,
Paignton front jacket inset bottom left, title page, 6–7, 27, 66–67, 68, 72, 93,
112–113, 114, 131, 147 top, centre top, centre bottom, bottom, 182–183,
215, 217; Moorfield Aquatics, Barnoldswick 122–123; Natural History Photo-
graphic Agency, Hythe – J. & M. Bain 177; Natural History Photographic
Agency – G.J. Cambridge 20; Natural History Photographic Agency – F.
Greenaway 180; Natural History Photographic Agency – M. Savonius 60–61;
Spectrum Colour Library, London 15 top, 77; D.P. Wilson/Eric and David
Hosking, London 8 left, 8 right, 19 left, 19 right, 20 inset, 28 top, 74, 92, 95
bottom; Z.E.F.A., London – Richard Nicholas front jacket inset top, 194–195.

*Illustrations are by* Fred'k St. Ward, Ralph Stobart

Some of the illustrations in this book have formerly appeared in *A Guide to The
Seashore, Beachcombing and Beachcraft, Botanic Man, Life in the Sea, My World of
Nature,* and *The Hamlyn All-Colour Animal Encyclopedia* all published by The
Hamlyn Publishing Group Limited.

# Contents

# Introduction

The narrow necklet of beauty we call the seashore is extremely fragile, and today it is threatened on all sides. Promenades and jetties are built on its upper limits, while bathing pools, marinas and harbours also cover parts of the natural shore. We all like these facilities, but there is a need to conserve parts of our coastline in its original natural form.

Today, this is being done by various organizations, and by the establishment of coastal nature reserves and country parks. However,

The natural beauty of a beach spoiled by stranded rubbish.

in spite of the obvious care taken by people, the tide line is changing rapidly, and today there is not a beach in the world that does not have its quota of plastic rubbish. The rubbish is there because unthinking people threw it away from ships and picnics, or it was simply dropped by accident. Not much of it affects the creatures and plants of the seashore, but it is very unsightly and spoils the beauty of our beaches.

But surely, the main problem is oil. Its clinging misery floats on the seas and kills thousands of seabirds every year; it comes ashore and kills vast numbers of seashore plants and animals; it coats the sand with its black filth and we get it on our clothes and shoes.

The seashore is one of the few really natural places left in our crowded environment, and naturalists throughout the world are striving to keep it that way. I hope that you, as a seashore naturalist, will care enough about the beauty and wonder of the seashore to do all you are able, to conserve its clean, natural life.

## Tides

As you walk along various shores, you will notice that the tide line is never in the same place at the same time, two days following. It varies from day to day, and according to where you are, may be rising higher or falling back.

This tidal movement forms a rhythm which is controlled by the gravitational pull of the Moon. This pull occurs at every point on the Earth. On the side of the Earth nearest the Moon, there is a greater pull on the water than on the Earth itself, thus causing a high tide. On the other side of the Earth, there is less pull on the water than on the Earth, so the water is 'left behind' thus causing a high tide. Since the Earth rotates once every 24 hours, there are two high tides per 24 hours.

Because the Moon also circles the Earth, the time between high and low water is not exactly six hours, but closer to 6·25 hours. So it is that each day the times of the high tides varies by about one hour.

The position of the Moon also causes variation in the heights of high

If you stand on the shore and watch the tide rise, you will notice the water coming up the beach. It is not so obvious that it is also rising vertically. *Below left:* Low tide in an estuary, and the rocks are exposed. *Below right:* High tide, and the rocks are covered.

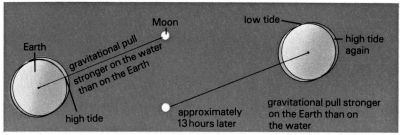

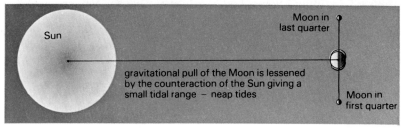

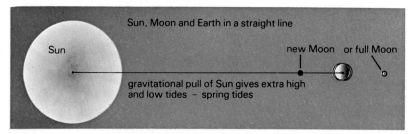

*Above:* The effect of the Moon on tidal movement
*Below:* The effect of the Sun on tidal movement

tides. At the time of new Moon and full Moon, the Sun, Earth and Moon are in a straight line so there is an even greater gravitational pull. The sea therefore rises very high up the shore and goes a long way out. These are called spring tides. After new and full Moon, the tides dwindle until, a week later, they move only a short distance up and down the shore. These are called neap tides.

This movement of the tides is a big factor in influencing where plants and animals live on the shore, because the amount of time they are underwater varies with the tide.

A knowledge of tides is important to a seashore naturalist. Not only is it necessary to know the times of high and low tides, but it is necessary to know when low spring tides occur so that you know when the maximum amount of shore is uncovered.

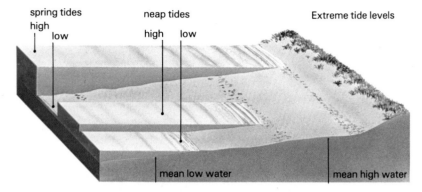

spring tides  
high  
low  

neap tides  
high  low  

Extreme tide levels

mean low water | mean high water

The distance the tide moves up the beach and down again changes daily. Peak movement occurs on spring tides, minimum movement on neap tides.

Fortunately, we can buy tide timetables which give us all this information. They can be bought from some newsagents, harbour masters, yachting stores, ships' chandlers and fishing tackle and sports shops.

If we follow a single tide as it ebbs (goes out) we can name the various regions of the shore. At the highest point where plants and animals live is the splash zone, so called because it is the area where only wave splashes reach. Next is a wide band called the upper shore which lies between extreme spring high water and extreme neap high water. Then comes the middle shore lying between mean (average) high water and mean low water. Finally comes the lower shore, and this stretches from middle shore to the part that is never uncovered – the sea itself.

The different regions of the shore. Each region has different characteristics, and therefore different animals or plants living there.

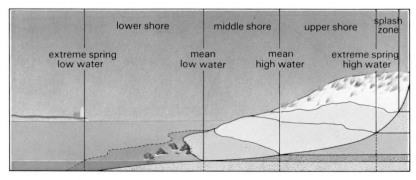

lower shore | middle shore | upper shore | splash zone

extreme spring low water | mean low water | mean high water | extreme spring high water

limpets

mussel

whelk

## Seashore code for naturalists

1. Remember that your feet can damage and destroy. Walk carefully.
2. Always replace rocks carefully after looking under them. Many creatures live there.
3. Collect only empty shells and dead animals.
4. If you take away living animals for examination in your aquarium, always return them later to the same place or a similar habitat.
5. Be a conservationist. Help to conserve the natural coastline and seashore, and protect it in every possible way.
6. Do not forget that the tide turns. Do not get stranded by a rising tide.

Each type of living space is usually occupied by some kind of animal. Each is well adapted with survival techniques, to suit its habitat.

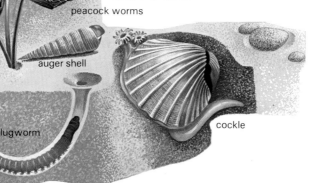

peacock worms

auger shell

lugworm

cockle

# Rocky shores

Most rocky shores have their share of rock pools which vary in size from tiny saucer-sized depressions to large pools over a metre in depth. They also vary in position from the top of the shore to the very edge of low tide.

Those near the top of the shore are subject to more changes in conditions than those lower down, but all rock pools experience daily, nightly and seasonal changes in salinity and temperature.

Imagine a small rock pool. It is early morning with bright sunlight, and the tide is ebbing. The water in the pool has just been renewed by the sea that covered it, and it is the same temperature as the sea. As the sun climbs higher, the water in the pool rises in temperature. Due to this, and the effect of the winds, a

Rocky shores of all kinds are to be found around the coasts. Here, under rocks, in crevices, gullies and beneath the seaweed curtains are to be found a rich host of plants and animals, in dazzling variety.

slow evaporation begins. The water in the pool becomes both warmer and saltier.

If there is a shower of rain, there may be a very sudden change in the salinity and temperature of the pool, but as the day passes, the water will certainly become warmer. Eventually, the tide returns, and within the space of a few minutes, the temperature of the pool plunges. At night, the green plants are not giving off oxygen, but the animals continue to need oxygen and are still giving off carbon dioxide. The plants are not using up the carbon dioxide nor giving off oxygen because they do not photosynthesize at night when there is no sunlight. So there is a steady build-up of carbon dioxide which tends to make the water rather acid. These constant changes within the pool have to be tolerated by the animals and plants living there, and rock pool life varies according to the position of the pool on the shore, because of the different conditions.

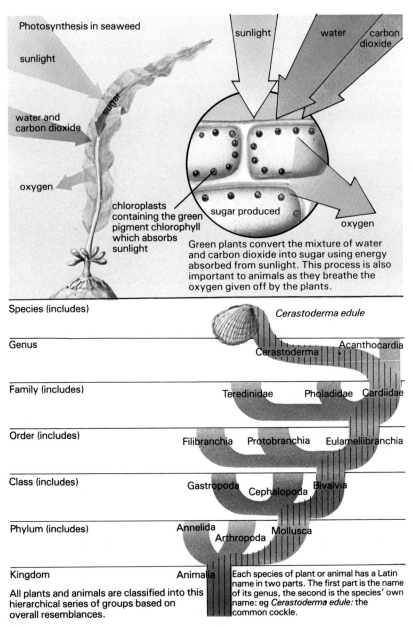

Photosynthesis in seaweed

sunlight

sunlight    water    carbon dioxide

water and carbon dioxide

sugar

oxygen

chloroplasts containing the green pigment chlorophyll which absorbs sunlight

sugar produced

oxygen

Green plants convert the mixture of water and carbon dioxide into sugar using energy absorbed from sunlight. This process is also important to animals as they breathe the oxygen given off by the plants.

Species (includes)     *Cerastoderma edule*

Genus     *Cerastoderma*     Acanthocardia

Family (includes)     Teredinidae     Pholadidae     Cardiidae

Order (includes)     Filibranchia     Protobranchia     Eulamellibranchia

Class (includes)     Gastropoda     Cephalopoda     Bivalvia

Phylum (includes)     Annelida     Arthropoda     Mollusca

Kingdom     Animalia

All plants and animals are classified into this hierarchical series of groups based on overall resemblances.

Each species of plant or animal has a Latin name in two parts. The first part is the name of its genus, the second is the species' own name: eg *Cerastoderma edule:* the common cockle.

If you want to discover all the different animals in a rock pool, you will have to watch quietly and keep quite still. Every few minutes, you will spot something moving over the bottom. Perhaps a small green shore crab will scuttle from one cover to another, or a prawn will dance daintily over the sand, pausing every few steps to examine a food possibility.

If you search carefully, you will find many animals in a rock pool. *Below*: This one contains mussels, limpets, periwinkles, anemones, a sea-slug and a crab.

## Anemones

Let's start with a pool near the top of the shore. The pool is probably lined with pink *Lithophyllum* and thickets of *Corallina* seaweeds (see page 44). A search may reveal the snakelocks anemone (*Anemonia sulcata*), with its greenish-grey tentacles spread wide and writhing to catch food. Flower-like they may be, but in fact, anemones are hungry animals catching their prey with poison tentacles.

Each tentacle is armed with many tiny cells, rather like microscopic barrels. Along the outer edge of each of these is a trigger mechanism, and a microscopic length of tissue ending in a poison barb. It's just like a miniature harpoon and rope. Immediately a fish touches any of these tentacles, the triggers fire and the barbs shoot into the body of the fish, each carrying a tiny injection of poison. Held both by the 'ropes' and affected by the poison, the fish is soon dead and being eaten by the anemone.

In some pools, you may find a variety of snakelocks with very attractive pink tips to the tentacles.

If you take some small pieces of fish down to the shore with you, you can place a piece on the tentacle tips and watch the animal feed. You will see it draw the food slowly inwards towards its mouth which is in the centre, and finally, the piece

Cross-section of an anemone.

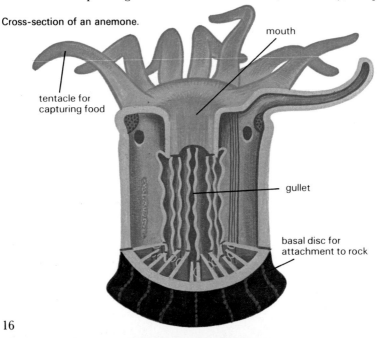

mouth

tentacle for capturing food

gullet

basal disc for attachment to rock

This dahlia anemone has used its stinging tentacles to catch a blenny.

of fish will disappear completely as the anemone swallows it.

Along the edge of such pools you will see the blood red, brown or green beadlet anemone (*Actinia equina*) and occasionally one spotted like a strawberry, and called the strawberry form because of its likeness to the fruit. These species are quite common on the upper shore.

Beadlets may look very static animals, but they are quite active and move very slowly from one place to another. If, in so doing, they touch another beadlet, a piece of rather astonishing behaviour begins. The larger of the two anemones first withdraws the tentacles that touched the other. Then, slowly, it begins to grow upwards until it towers over the smaller one. At the same time,

the blue spots at the base of its tentacles swell up and the surrounding flesh grows into a collar which then begins to point out towards the small anemone. Quickly, the anemone bends over and strikes the smaller one with this collar, releasing spots of stinging cells on to the column of the smaller one. After this, the attacker returns to its normal shape. The injured anemone retreats and the areas where it was stung frequently become septic.

Generally, the red anemones are much more aggressive than the green. You may wonder about the reason for this behaviour. It is probable that it helps anemones to keep their distance, one from another, so they do not have to compete for food.

If you would like to see this behaviour happen, all you need to do is collect a large red anemone and a green one. It is quite safe to pick them up. Place them in your marine aquarium on separate flat stones well apart. Let them settle for two or three days, and then place the stones together so that the anemones touch one another. You will then see the whole sequence.

In pools near low tide limit, you may be able to find the beautiful dahlia anemone (*Tealia felina*). These grow quite large, and I have seen one with a disc the size of a tea-plate. They are usually a reddish brown colour with grey markings, but nearly white and also pink specimens can be found.

## Tube worms

As you look down into a pool, you will almost certainly see stones and shells with white worm-like growths on them. These are the limey homes of a tube-building worm (*Pomatoceros* spp) and each tube has a sort of keel running its entire length ending in a sharp spine. If you place a stone with some of these tubes on it, into a shallow pool and wait for a while, you may see the tips of the worms starting to come out. Their head end appears as a plumed crown of white tentacles, streaked and spotted with red and blue. But if you let a shadow fall across them, or disturb the water, they will immediately withdraw into their tubes.

Many of the tubes you examine will be pure white towards the open end, whereas the thinner end will be covered in algae. This is because the worm has recently enlarged its tube-home and algal growth has not yet started. You will probably notice too, that the tube is shaped like a very elongated ice cream cone. When the worm started making the tube, it was small, and as the worm grew, so it needed to enlarge the tube.

All materials that the worm needs for the construction of such a tube are taken from the seawater, and the food it eats.

Some of the seaweeds are often speckled with the tiny spiral tube worm (*Spirorbis* spp). It's about 3 to 5 millimetres in diameter and two species can be recognized by the direction of the coiled tube. *Spirorbis borealis* is rolled clockwise, whereas *Spirorbis spirillum* is rolled in an anti-clockwise direction.

## Barnacles

In and around the pools will be hundreds of barnacles (*Chthamalus* and *Balanus* spp). They are crusta-

Barnacles and tube worms cement themselves down on to shells and stones on the seabed.

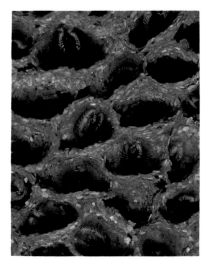

*Left*: Heads of reef building tube worms *Sabellaria alveolata* can be seen at the open end of the tubes. *Right*: A worm removed from its tube.

ceans, related to crabs, and settle out of the plankton and become cemented to the rock surface. When the tide covers them, each one starts to stick out a net-like foot which arcs through the water and catches drifting particles for food. They live for

as long as five years, and since each one is both male and female (hermaphrodite) each releases its quota of young into the sea. After a while, these larvae settle on to rocks and grow into adult barnacles.

To obtain some idea of the numbers of barnacles on a shore, try counting how many are in a 10 centimetre square. By multiplying up, you will begin to realize their vast numbers. There could be as many as 35000 in a square metre.

## Molluscs

### Limpets
Limpets (*Patella* and *Patina* spp) are often attached to the sides of rock pools, and, on rare occasions,

you may be fortunate enough to see one moving along. If the rocks near-by are covered with a felt-like growth of algae, search for the zig-zag feeding track of limpets. These are made as the animals' jaws rasp away at the algae as they move slowly forward, swinging their heads from side to side. At the same time, you will probably notice that where limpets are numerous, seaweeds are scarce. This is largely because they eat the young plants of many of them as they continually feed.

Did you know that limpets have a homing instinct? Each one lives more or less permanently in its spot on the rock. When the tide comes in and covers it, it begins to crawl about and feed. It may travel several metres away from its 'home', but when the tide turns, it makes its way back home, and pulls itself firmly down on to the rock surface. There, it remains until the next tide comes in and it sets off on its journeys once more.

Over the years it lives in the one place. The constant pulling down of the shell slowly wears away the rock and forms a scar – a depression. One day, the limpet will die, and only the scar will remain as a sign of where it once lived.

Common limpets, and scars where other limpets once lived. *Inset*: A limpet from underneath showing its large foot, head and tentacles.

## Hermit crab

Small hermit crabs (*Eupagurus bern-hardus*), although common in rock pools, usually hide beneath stones or behind seaweed. They are not molluscs, but they inhabit many different kinds of mollusc shells from periwinkles (*Littorina* spp) and dog whelks (*Nassarius* spp) to tower shells (*Turritella* spp). In fact, any univalve shell (a shell of one piece) of a suitable size serves them as a home. Some of the very young ones seem to live in pieces of tube worm casing, especially in early summer.

Hermit crabs will feed on pieces of fish, if you offer it. If you want to observe one really closely, find a large cockle or limpet shell; fill it with water, and place the hermit in it upside down. You will then be able to watch it as it tugs its shell around, and turns the right way up.

## Periwinkles

If you follow the tide down the shore, you will probably notice, here and there, some tiny yellow molluscs crawling over and among the sea-weed. Look a little more closely, and you will find some similar shells of a red, brown, black, a few white and occasionally some red chequerboard patterns. All these are colour varieties of the flat periwinkle (*Littorina littoralis*). They feed on the seaweed, and the dampness among the fronds, combined with the shelter the fronds provide, makes ideal living conditions for this small member of the periwinkle family.

## Finding members of the periwinkle family

If you are on a rocky shore which has a large space between the high and low tide marks, see if you can find *all* the members of the periwinkle family. There are only four species to discover. Largest member of the family is the common periwinkle (*Littorina littorea*) commonly called the edible periwinkle, because it is so good to eat.

The shells are sharply pointed and vary in colour from black to brown and reddish-brown, and they are always patterned with darker concentric lines. A few specimens may be striped greyish-yellow and black. They will be found congregating together on small stones and rocks on the middle shore and below. Their numbers are very high on some shores, and it is there the winkle gatherers go to harvest them. Yet, in spite of such predation, the edible periwinkle is very common, and this is most surely the result of its highly successful survival techniques.

In rough weather, the animal withdraws into its shell, shuts the 'door' and simply allows itself to be rolled about by the waves. Its stout shell is proof against the roughest of storms. When exposed by an ebb tide, the edible periwinkle produces a mucus which spreads over the rock and the open edge of the shell then dries and 'glues' the periwinkle to the rock. Even when exposed to very hot sun, this sealing of the shell prevents the evaporation of moisture from within, and so the mollusc remains quite healthy in very adverse conditions.

Another member of this family is the rough periwinkle (*Littorina saxatilis*) and this one lives between half tide level right up to the splash zone. Its shell is very roughly ribbed and may be brown, red, black or yellow. If you scratch the surface of the shell with your thumb nail, you will detect this roughness which distinguishes it from the edible periwinkle.

The third member, the flat periwinkle (*Littorina littoralis*), has already been dealt with at the beginning of this section.

Fourthly, and most difficult to find, is the tiny, small periwinkle (*Littorina neritoides*). You must search for this one in narrow grooves in the rock or cliff face in the splash zone, sometimes among, but usually above, the tufted growths of the seaweed called channelled wrack (*Pelvetia canaliculata*), (see page 37). The shell, as little as 3 millimetres long,

Every region of a rocky shore is inhabited by one of the members of the periwinkle family. Each species has adapted to conditions in different regions.

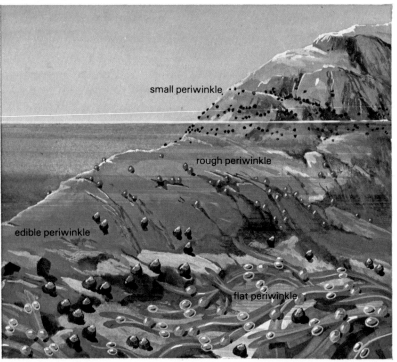

is thin with a bluish haze over its light brown colour. Search in the narrowest of crevices, and you will need a pin or pointed matchstick to prise it out.

## Top-shells

Nearly as common as the periwinkles are the various species of top-shells, which are generally less rounded. The thick top-shell (*Gibbula lineata* sometimes referred to as *Monodonta lineata*) is about 2·5 centimetres high and is found on the middle shore. The shell is grey-green with purple zig-zags and the inside edge of the aperture (open end) is silvery mother of pearl.

Another top-shell known as the grey top-shell (*Gibbula cineraria*), is sometimes referred to as silver tommy, due to many specimens having part of the shell eroded to expose the silver nacre (mother-of-pearl) beneath. You can easily recognize this species by this silver colouration. It is about 1·25 centimetres high and is found mainly on the middle and lower shore.

Very much like the silver tommy, but much flatter and of a purplish colour, is the purple top-shell (*Gibbula umbilicalis*) found on the middle to lower shore.

Search under ledges and behind seaweed curtains for the beautiful painted top-shell (*Calliostoma zizyphinum*). You will find it in particular near low spring tide level, on the underside of a crevice among sponges and sea squirts. Its shell is yellow or

pink with reddish streaks and with its straight sides and pointed spire, it is unmistakeable. In the spring, you may be fortunate to find its egg ribbons in such places.

## Cowries

A very distinctive little univalve (an animal with a shell of one piece) to be found on the underside of ledges near low tide marks is the cowrie (*Trivia* spp). Less than a centimetre long, it is brownish-purple above and pale below. It feeds on sea-squirts, and where it is common, the empty cowrie shells can be collected on the tide line.

## Boring shellfish

Every available space on the shore is taken over by *some* species, and the interior of rocks is no exception. Some of the most efficient borers into rock are the piddocks (*Pholadidea, Barnea, Pholas* and *Zirfaea* spp).

All of them bore mechanically and are found in a variety of rocks, although they are usually most numerous in the softer rocks such as sandstones, shales and chalk. On beaches where ancient forests are submerged, they bore into the now soft wood of the old root systems.

The shell of a piddock is a highly efficient drill with a row of teeth at one end. The foot is large and acts as a sucker organ to attach the mollusc to the end of the burrow. Turning first to one side and then to another, the piddock slowly wears away the rock. As it grows, so it makes a larger burrow, and in this it is 'trapped' because when it started boring on the outer surface of the rock, it was tiny. Once it has started growing, it cannot escape through its small entrance. Completely protected, it lives its entire life within the rock. Some species are even luminous, although the reason for this is not yet known.

To find piddocks, search rock surfaces for holes up to 15 millimetres in diameter. If you tap the rock surface hard with a stone, you will see a jet of water erupt from some of the holes. This is a sure sign a piddock is at home.

## Crabs and lobsters

### Crabs of the rocky shore

There are so many different species of crab living on the shore, each with its own way of life, that an entire book could be devoted to them.

Green shore crabs (*Carcinus maenas*) populate most rocky shores in large numbers, and are to be found on both N. European and Mediterranean coastlines.

**How crabs grow** Like all crabs, a green shore crab grows by moulting, i.e. by casting away its old, hard covering. At various times throughout the year, the crab's armour splits and lifts the rear part of the back. Through this split, the crab slowly draws out its body: legs come out from leg coverings, feelers from their hard coats, and even the eyes are pulled free from their transparent covers. The total skin cast takes from 2 to 4 hours.

Finally, the crab is free of its old suit of armour. But now its body is soft and it must hide away for as long as 14 days during which time its body swells in size (i.e. it grows) and its covering hardens.

A large number of the crab 'shells' to be found on the shore result from the cast skins of growing crabs.

**Life history of a crab** Crabs are either male or female and the sexes can be distinguished as follows. Turn the crab upside down and look at its 'purse' i.e. the turned-in tail flap at the rear end. A *narrow* triangular 'purse' is a male; the *broader based* triangular 'purse' is a female.

A few days before a female moults, the male crab clasps her to his underside and carries her around for several days during which time he fertilizes her eggs. Some time afterwards, the 150 000 or more eggs are laid and become attached to hairs beneath her purse.

The eggs are carried for several months and you will certainly find crabs in this condition, and the eggs can be plainly seen. You may occasionally come upon a pair of crabs too. In due time, the eggs hatch and tiny spiked larvae are released into the plankton in the sea. There, they undergo changes until, finally, looking rather like tiny transparent crabs, they settle on the seabed.

**Survival** A green shore crab is a multi-purpose crab, hardy and

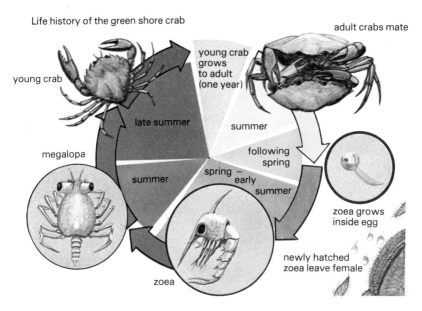

Life history of the green shore crab

adult crabs mate

young crab grows to adult (one year)

young crab

late summer

summer

megalopa

following spring

summer

spring – early summer

zoea grows inside egg

newly hatched zoea leave female

zoea

*Below*: A female shore crab showing the mass of eggs it is carrying.

possessing a variety of survival techniques. For instance, it frequently hides away in narrow crevices; it is equally at home beneath rocks; it is common amongst seaweed where it shelters against the holdfasts; in rock pools it burrows into the sand to avoid predators. You will pick them up beneath ledges, find them in your prawn net and catch them in drop nets.

If stranded in small rock pools where the oxygen content drops very low, these crabs come up to the edge of the pool, and raise part of their bodies out of the water to breathe through the surface area.

Their colour patterns tend to change according to where they live. For instance, young ones well up the shore among bright pieces of shell and stones, have dazzle patterns of red, black and white amongst their usual green colour. Such youngsters can actually change colour to suit the environment, although it's a slow change taking several hours to a few days.

Larger shore crabs can still change colour, but it takes very much longer. Nevertheless, most green shore crabs found among the green seaweeds are green and yellow, whereas those found in deeper water, where red seaweeds are common, have a general reddish brown colour.

Because it can stand a variety of salinities, the shore crab will also be found quite high in estuaries where freshwater content is high. It's a very successful species.

**The senses of crabs** Crabs are aware of their surroundings through the senses of sight, touch, smell and taste. Their eyes are quite sensitive to movement of all kinds, especially shadows – after all, a moving shadow could be a fish or bird swooping to seize them!

The sense of touch works through the many small hairs on various parts of the body which receive vibrations coming through the water from all kinds of moving objects. They can even taste with their legs, through special areas which detect food.

**New limbs for old** Because crabs live in a rocky environment where storms tumble stones around, they frequently get their limbs trapped. Also, they fight and lose limbs. However, this represents no problem to a crab, as it simply regrows or regenerates the damaged or lost limb.

You will often find a crab with one or more legs missing, and a small stump where the new one is growing. Sometimes, you will find one with a small nipper claw less than half the size of the normal one. After a few moults, the new leg will be full size once again.

**A rich variety of crabs** The most ferocious of all crabs to be found on the shore is the velvet swimming crab (*Portunus puber*). It grows up to 8 centimetres long. It is red-brown, although a covering of fine hair gives it a muddy colour. Its reaction to disturbance is to sit back and lift its nipper claws, snapping them rapidly to warn you off. Be careful how you pick one of these up. They really are quick! Their rear legs have flattened paddle-like ends, which act as oars to push them through the water in quite rapid swimming action.

Velvet swimming crabs swim quickly up through the sea to catch small fish in midwater. You will find them fairly low on the shore, hiding away beneath rocks and clumps of seaweed.

One or two species of porcelain-crab (*Porcellana* spp) are very numerous on some shores. They are quite unmistakeable, as they cling flatly to the underside of rocks, their rather hairy bodies well covered with sediment. Large flat nipper claws and their comparatively small size (up to 1 centimetre) help you to identify them. Be careful if you handle them – their nipper claws break off very easily.

Small hairy crabs (*Pilumnus hirtellus*) live in spaces among the stones and broken shells beneath rocks. They are brownish-red, and as their name suggests, they are hairy and this makes them easy to identify.

The young of edible crabs (*Cancer*

This shore crab is regrowing the claw on the right. It will take several moults before the claw becomes as large as the original one.

*pagurus*) up to 50 millimetres wide, will also be found in such hideaways. If you pick one up, it folds all its legs tightly over its abdomen, and refuses to move, until it feels assured all danger has passed. Larger specimens can sometimes be found under wide rock ledges, but they are almost impossible to get out. They simply press their backs against the roof and defy all your efforts. They are indeed very strong.

An exciting find might be a very large spiny spider crab (*Maia squinado*). They are reddish in colour and big ones can reach the size of a flattened melon with a leg span of nearly 1 metre. They are rare on the shore, but over the years, I have come upon several of them.

**Master of camouflage** Very much smaller (about 1·5 centimetres

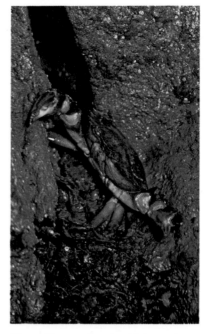

*Above*: Shore crabs retreat into crevices and defend themselves with spread claws.

*Below*: A spiny spider crab dressed up with seaweed as camouflage.

across) and a little easier to find, is the small spider crab (*Macropodia* spp) with legs fragile and thin as pins. They are difficult to see because they dress themselves up with small pieces of seaweed. To do this, they nip off pieces with their claws, hold them to their mouths and chew the ends of the seaweed before 'planting' it on to the spines and hairs that cover parts of their body.

If you put one of these in a tank after gently removing all the weed and give it a small plant of any red seaweed to crawl amongst, you will be able to watch it dress up. Within a few hours, it will be almost indistinguishable from the plant. It is an excellent example of camouflage, because it uses the plant on which it is living to blend it in and help it 'disappear'.

## Lobsters

Often when you lift a stone near low tide mark, you will hear a distinct and continued flapping noise, and usually, see a disturbance among the seaweed. This will be a squat lobster (*Galathea* spp), looking rather like a small lobster. They are fierce little creatures, so be careful how you pick them up. Incidentally, when you put it down again, you will see the cause of the sound you heard, for it uses its tail to flip backwards and retreat into cover.

Common Lobsters (*Homarus vulgaris*) are not very common on the shore, and remember, they are blue when alive.

## Fish of the shore

Your first acquaintance with a shore fish will probably be little more than a momentary sighting – a mere flash – as it swims from one piece of cover to another.

To survive on the shore, a fish has to move very fast. To move about, it must wait for the lull between waves and dart a few centimetres to a safe place and then hold on with all its fins whilst the next wave breaks. As a result of this hectic life, shore fish have fins modified and stiffened to act as 'grippers', to help them wedge themselves into tiny crevices and beneath rocks.

### Sea scorpions

Most formidable of the shore fish are undoubtedly the father lasher or bullhead (*Cottus scorpius*) and the long-spined sea scorpion (*Cottus bubalis*). They are fascinating fish with enormous mouths spread across very large flattened heads, and have sharp spines sticking out from their gill covers. These can give you an unpleasant prick if you pick up a sea scorpion carelessly. The father lasher can grow to 20 centimetres long. The long-spined sea scorpion is slightly smaller.

Their method of feeding is unusual too. They lie in wait, their brown-grey bodies beautifully camouflaged against a rock face or among seaweed. Keeping perfectly still, they are very patient, and their eyes do not miss a single movement in the water nearby. If a small fish, crab or prawn approaches too close, the sea scorpion jerks forward and its enormous mouth swallows the prey with a rat-trap-like snap.

If you come upon one and have some pieces of fish with you, offer it a piece and you will see the fantastic gobbling action for yourself. Occasionally, you will catch one when prawning, and then you will see its defensive action. It gapes wide with its mouth, and this movement both makes the spines stick out and its head enlarge to nearly twice the size. Such a defensive action must be useful when it is attacked or seized by a seabird – it would most certainly make it very difficult to swallow.

## Blennies

Blennies (Blenniidae) are attractive shore fish and you will find them sheltering in the damp, beneath rocks when the tide is out. They have thick-lipped mouths, and sharp teeth, ideally suited to biting into barnacles, which are their staple food. Their large eyes and lively manner together with their habit of investigating everything that moves near to them, makes them the most likeable fish to be found on the shore.

As you turn over a rock, the presence of a blenny may at first not be detected, for they do lie still when first threatened. Within a few seconds, it will start flipping about with gymnastic skill, springing its body so rapidly that individual

movements cannot be seen. Watch and wait and it will come to rest, and then, with dampened hands, you will be able to gently pick it up. Have a good look, and then return it, for the warmth of your hand is not good for a blenny's well-being.

In late spring to early summer, the male undergoes a startling colour change, and becomes a jet black with whitish lips. This is his courtship dress, and afterwards, when the female has laid her eggs, he remains guard over them. His fierce appearance evidently keeps predators well away.

## Butterfish

Another attractive little shore fish, frequently to be found under stones or drifts of seaweed is the butterfish (*Centronotus gunnellus*). I have usually found this fish curled up in upturned cockle and scallop shells. This preference for shells may be connected with its habit of egg laying in shells, although sometimes they lay eggs in rock crevices and holes made by rock boring molluscs. It's a fairly easy species to recognize, because it has a rather long and eel-like body (up to 20 centimetres) with a series of black spots along its entire length.

## Gobies

A family of fish easily confused with blennies are the gobies (Gobiidae). When you first spot a small fish jumping around, as you lift a rock, it is most difficult to identify. Similarly, in rock pools, a fish darting from cover may easily be a blenny *or* a goby.

Generally speaking, gobies have slimmer bodies with separated fins along the back, whereas blennies are bigger bodied in front and taper towards the tail, with a continuous fin line along the back. Gobies have a more 'pop eyed' appearance and blennies thicker lips. But like so many aspects of identification, it becomes easier, the more familiar you become with each species.

Usually, you will be able to spot them as they move, for they swim with sudden short bursts and then stop. When they *do* stop, they literally merge into their background.

Gobies are not the easiest little fish to watch, but with patience you may see one dart forward to seize some food item. If you drop a few tiny pieces of fish into a pool inhabited by gobies, they will very soon detect your offering and you will see them come after it.

There are many different species of goby, but only one is free swimming in open water. This is the spotted goby (*Gobius ruthensparri*), and you may see small shoals of this little fish 'hovering' in open water among seaweeds, or cruising very slowly in deep pools. Incidentally, because of this habit, it makes an excellent aquarium inhabitant.

Spotted gobies swim in small shoals among seaweed. The other species of goby live on the bottom.

## Marine stickleback

A really fascinating fish occasionally caught in prawn nets is the sea stickleback or fifteen-spined stickleback (*Spinachia vulgaris*). It prefers pools, but on a few occasions, I have found one in the shallows beneath rocks. It has a most distinctive shape, with a very thin body tapering to a large tail, but most noticeable is its long, tube-like head which ends in a small, upturned mouth rather like that of a pipefish (see page 94).

It's a fish with a most interesting nesting habit, and I have kept them in early spring, simply to watch their courtship and egg-laying behaviour. At such times of the year, males are much darker than the females, and the females' bodies are usually very distended with eggs. They look literally as if they are going to 'burst'!

Courtship consists of the male approaching a female and performing a series of mouth proddings along her flank. He becomes extremely aggressive towards any other male that comes into his territory. The territory in the breeding season is usually a small area of seaweed with one or more stiffish up-growing seaweed plant. These are selected as the nest site.

The male then swims around the area, marking it here and there with match-head sized white blobs of jelly, which he secretes and sticks to seaweed fronds.

Then comes the time to build the nest. He swims up to a seaweed plant, often a red species, and begins to pull at pieces of the plant, tugging hard as he grips it in his mouth. Eventually he succeeds in breaking it off and then he swims back to the nest site, where he pushes it between the fronds of the growing plant. After many journeys, a lemon-sized mass of loose pieces is built up. Sometime later, he begins to trail from his vent a semi-transparent gelatinous thread. Swimming close to the nest, he begins to bind it together by going round and round, as the thread is pulled from his body. The threads criss-cross and he continually varies his course until the nest is thoroughly enmeshed in a network of threads, which appear to tighten as they 'dry'. A few long threads are led out like tent guy ropes to nearby rocks, and other parts of the plant.

It's an amazing sight to watch and the total length of thread secreted by his kidneys is many metres long.

Finally, he persuades his mate to come down and swim into the nest where she leaves her eggs and then swims away, leaving him on guard. He takes his duties very seriously, and seldom strays more than half a metre from the nest and eggs. If any intruder comes near, he rushes at it and drives it away.

This is something you can observe for yourself, providing you set up a small aquarium and are able to catch a male and female stickleback to put in it.

## Sponges and sea-squirts

If you look under ledges and rock overhangs, at low spring tide level, you will find the surfaces coated with sponges. They are animals that live together in colonies and simply syphon in seawater, take out food particles, and pass out the cleaned water. There are many different kinds. One common one to be found is the purse sponge (*Grantia compressa*), a collection of small bag-like sponges often attached to seaweed.

A sponge

The passage of water through a sponge. Water enters through small pores.

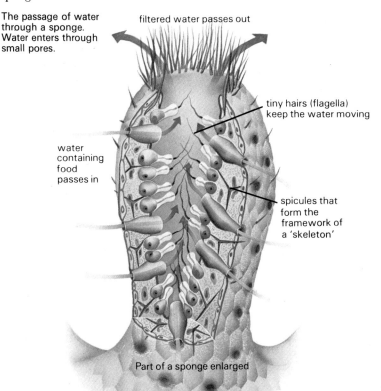

filtered water passes out

tiny hairs (flagella) keep the water moving

water containing food passes in

spicules that form the framework of a 'skeleton'

Part of a sponge enlarged

An orange-yellow sponge is the sulphur sponge (*Suberites domuncula*) but most common of all in many areas is the breadcrumb sponge (*Halichondria panicea*), which looks like a collection of tiny greyish-yellow volcanoes all tightly matted together – and not very much like breadcrumbs!

Sea-squirts (Ascidiacea) like *Ciona intestinalis*, raise their transparent flask-like bodies among the rocks. They, too, syphon feed and the most beautiful of these is surely the star ascidian (*Botryllus schlosseri*). Its bluish body spreads flatly over rocks, and sometimes on seaweed, and its lovely golden stars are plain to see. Each star is in fact a group of 3 to 12 individuals which feed individually, but share a common opening to pass water out.

*Ascidia mentula* is another kind of sea-squirt which grows up to 10 centimetres high. It is translucent green.

Inside view of a sea-squirt.

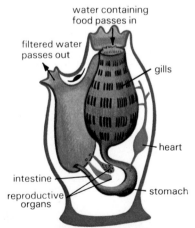

water containing
food passes in

filtered water
passes out

gills

heart

intestine

reproductive
organs

stomach

## Sea urchins and starfish

Sea urchins (Echinoidea) are easy to recognize because they have bodies covered with spines. Many are beautiful, all are interesting, and they are plentiful on most rocky shores. In Europe, the green sea urchin (*Psammechinus miliaris*) is quite numerous. It is sometimes called the purple-tipped sea urchin and this name describes it exactly. Look for it beneath stones, but often it is covered with shells and pebbles which it attaches to its body with its long tube feet.

If you turn one upside down, you will see the five small teeth with which it rasps away at vegetation, or feeds on fragments of animals.

Both in the Mediterranean and N. Europe, another urchin with a long name is *Paracentrotus lividus*, commonly known as the rock-urchin. It is around 5 centimetres across and usually green or brown in colour. But an urchin with a really long name is *Strongylocentrotus droebachiensis*. That is the name of a small green urchin with spines often less than 3 millimetres in length!

Related to the urchins are the starfish (Asteroidea). Usually with five arms, they are able to regenerate damaged or lost arms as can crabs. As you explore the seashore, you will almost certainly come across starfish with one or more tiny stubs of arms. Some species are pests on oyster beds and a story is told of how

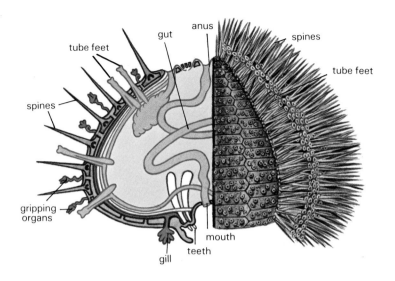

spines

tube feet

gut

anus

spines

tube feet

spines

gripping
organs

gill

mouth

teeth

A cut-away section of a sea urchin shows the intricate structure.

fishermen used to tow ropes behind their boats to ensnare the starfish without damaging the oysters. Once in the boat, the starfish were cut into pieces and thrown back, presumably dead. Unfortunately the fishermen did not realize that they were actually *increasing* the number of starfish! It was only when scientists discovered that, providing a portion of the central disc remains attached to the arm, a damaged starfish can regrow its limbs, that fishermen realized their mistake. It is a good example of how scientific knowledge helps the fishermen.

The cushion star (*Asterina gibbosa*) is to be found on the underside of rocks, and rock pools will often have other species in them, some stranded

from deeper water.

The common starfish (*Asterias rubens*) of European waters, feeds on bivalves. Below tidemark, it hunts molluscs such as the queen scallop (*Chlamys opercularis*) which, if it is successful in hunting, it clasps in its five arms. Slowly, it pulls the two shell valves apart and as soon as there is a gap of a few millimetres, it turns its own stomach inside out and pushes it inside the shell. It then digests the body of the captured scallop externally.

The body of the spiny starfish (*Marthasterias glacialis*) is covered with small spines, but in spite of all you may have heard, it is *not* (nor is any starfish) poisonous.

Remember that every rocky shore

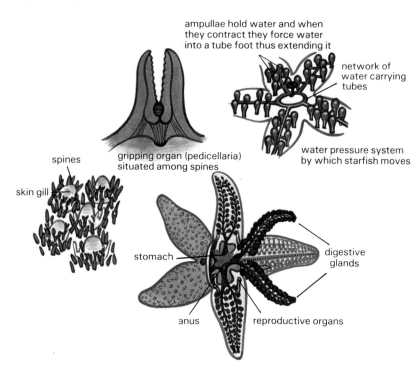

ampullae hold water and when they contract they force water into a tube foot thus extending it

network of water carrying tubes

gripping organ (pedicellaria) situated among spines

water pressure system by which starfish moves

spines

skin gill

stomach

digestive glands

anus

reproductive organs

Structure of a starfish. If you examine one closely with a hand lens, you will see details of its intricate spines and delicate tube feet.

has its own selection of plants and animals. No two shores are alike, and that is surely the best possible reason for exploring as many shores as you can.

## Seaweeds

If you look at the plants we call seaweeds covering the rocky shore, you will almost certainly notice that they have a very different habit of growth to those plants found on the land.

One very obvious difference is that seaweeds lie flat, draped limply over one another, whereas most land plants have an upright habit.

A reason for this becomes fairly obvious as soon as you begin to think about the environment in which seaweeds live. It may well be a calm, summer's day when you visit the shore, but when a storm blows up, huge waves crash down upon these plants, hurling stones and sand amongst them and exerting all kinds of pressures.

They have a further problem to cope with: how to conserve moisture. Even on a calm day there are drying breezes and the warmth of the sun takes moisture from the seaweeds too. Many of those on the upper shore will be left 'high and dry' for as long as 8 to 10 hours.

Like all plants, seaweeds need to feed and reproduce, and you will no doubt appreciate that these natural functions provide further problems which seaweeds have had to solve. So to survive on a rocky shore, these plants have to:

Conserve moisture;

Remain firmly fixed in place;

Be able to feed under varying conditions;

Have a reliable method of reproduction.

Let's see how seaweed is adapted, and how it copes with these conditions. There is no better way of finding out than by kneeling amongst them and actually touching them. As you rub your hand over them, the first sensation you have is one of slipperiness caused by the mucus which covers them. You probably realized just how slippery seaweed can be, when you first walked over it. In the same way that well-oiled machinery moves with a minimum of resistance, so one seaweed moves over another, and even over rock surfaces, with a minimum of friction and hence little damage.

Seaweeds have several ways of conserving moisture and the most obvious is to grow below the tidal zone or in rock pools. But many are successful because they hang like curtains in shaded gullies. Even those on the open rock faces are draped one over the other, thus finding shelter and allowing a steady spread of moisture from the underlying plants and rocks. Also, by lying flat, they offer less surface area to the drying winds.

It is on the top of the upper shore that the real problems begin, and if you look on rock surfaces around and just above high water mark, you will come across a seaweed called channelled wrack (*Pelvetia canaliculata*). The first thing you will notice is that it is small, with very thin fronds, and if you examine one of these fronds closely, you will discover another survival technique. The edges of the fronds are rolled inwards to form a sort of channel (hence the popular name) which is very nearly a complete tube. In this way, it prevents evaporation and so conserves moisture. It is a plant that needs to be able to do this because during spells of neap tides, it may have to survive as long as eight days without being submerged by the sea. During such periods, it becomes even smaller and quite hard to the touch, and changes to a black colour. But it only needs the splash from a few high tide waves to make it supple and soft once more, and to restore its deep green and dark yellow colours.

At the other extreme are the large oarweeds and tangles (Laminaria-

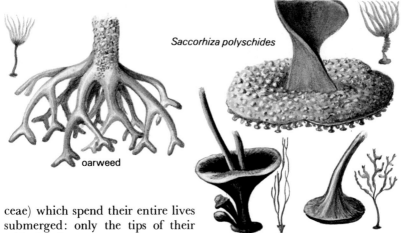

*Saccorhiza polyschides*

oarweed

sea-thong      bladder wrack

Seaweed holdfasts vary according to the species. Here are four main types.

ceae) which spend their entire lives submerged: only the tips of their wide fronds appear on the sea surface during the lowest of spring tides, and then only for about an hour.

Another major problem facing all seaweeds is the need to remain fixed, no matter what the weather conditions. Once again, if you examine one of the wracks, you will find the answer. Follow the fronds down to the rock face itself, and you will see the plant is attached by a disc-shaped mass. This is not a root however, and it does not feed like the roots of a tree. Instead, it is made up of a series of small shoots that grow in very close contact with the rough surface of the rock, and is called a holdfast. Just how efficient it is you will discover by pulling one of the plants with a sideways jerk. It certainly holds fast! But if you give it an extra strong wrench, it will come free, together with a wafer of rock, which proves the point even further.

Take a look at different kinds of seaweed, and with the aid of a hand lens, you will see how these plants are able to remain firm in the wildest of gales.

Since a seaweed spends a part of its life immersed in seawater, and seawater itself is a collection of many different minerals, feeding is fairly straightforward. It absorbs minerals through its fronds and in a way spends much of its life surrounded by a rich 'soup' of foods.

To help them maintain an upright position when covered by the sea, many seaweeds have air bladders on their fronds. Perhaps the best example of one is bladder wrack (*Fucus vesiculosus*) which has several of them, and if you squeeze one, you will hear it pop.

## Reproduction

To explain the reproduction of sea-weeds is no easy matter, for some of the methods are very complicated. However, it is possible to observe some of the more obvious reproductive parts, and a good example to use is knotted wrack.

The long fronds of knotted wrack (*Ascophyllum nodosum*) bear easily recognizable egg-shaped air bladders and growing out from these fronds are short branches which end in a rather flatter and worty bladder. Those on the male plants are a bright golden yellow, and those of the female plants much paler. They are called receptacles (or fruiting bodies) and they are divided into a large number of tiny compartments. Within these compartments are produced the male or female sex cells which when ripe are dispersed into the sea.

Life cycle of knotted wrack

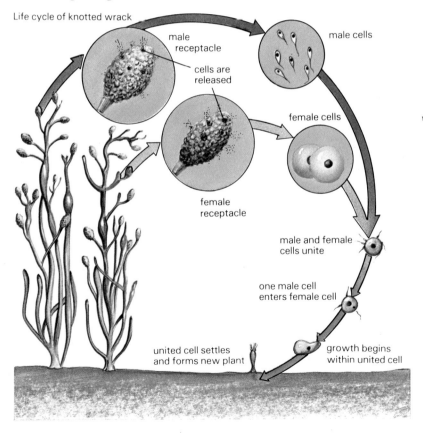

male receptacle

cells are released

male cells

female cells

female receptacle

male and female cells unite

one male cell enters female cell

united cell settles and forms new plant

growth begins within united cell

They are very tiny, and the sea is vast, but enough are released to ensure that a few meet and unite. This is made possible because the male cells swim, and if they come close to a female cell, they move immediately towards it. After a few minutes, there may be several male cells surrounding the female cell, but only one of the males penetrates the wall of the female cell and enters it. The others then fall away. Now growth begins within this united cell and eventually it will settle on the bottom to form a new plant. Other seaweeds reproduce by giving off spores, which more simply germinate into new seaweed plants.

## Seaweed colours

If you take a piece of bladder wrack and heat it in water, you will see that the water becomes quite brown. At the same time, the wrack will have changed to a green colour. This is simply because the brown is a colour pigment, which in the living seaweed covered the natural green of the plant. For, like all green plants, seaweeds contain chlorophyll, which, in the case of seaweeds, is usually obscured by pigments giving brown or red colours.

Sea-lettuce (*Ulva lactuca*) is quite a bright green, which is, of course, chlorophyll not covered by another colour. Incidentally, if you find pieces of cream or whitish coloured seaweeds, they are usually dead fragments that have been bleached due to loss of their normal colour.

## Seaweed zonation

The most important single factor in the seaweed's environment is the constant rhythm of the tides. Wherever the plant grows upon the shore, it will experience an ever-changing time of exposure when the tide is out. So, to survive on the shore, a seaweed plant has to be well equipped.

As an example, we can take a beach well covered with a thick growth of wracks. These wracks are perennials (i.e. they grow and live for a number of years), although many of them die early in life due to storms and the generally tough conditions under which they need to survive.

If you walk down the shore at low tide, you will notice that as you progress towards the sea, the species change. In fact, the seaweeds grow in zones or belts which are related to the various tide levels, and because this is so, it is referred to as zonation.

Highest on the shore will be channelled wrack growing as we have already seen, in tufts from high water mark down to the next zone, which is occupied by spiral wrack (*Fucus spiralis*). It can be recognized by its large receptacles which are not unlike sultanas. It has no air bladders and usually its fronds twist in a spiral fashion. On many beaches, it occupies quite a small zone, and is then followed by knotted wrack.

Mixed in with knotted wrack and extending down the shore, you will find serrated or saw wrack (*Fucus*

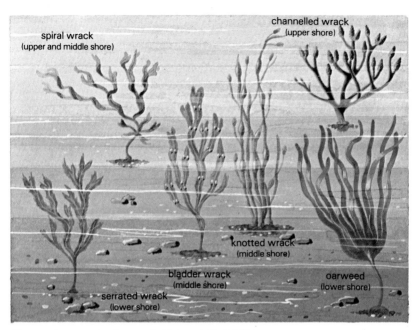

The wracks are a good example of seaweed zonation.

serratus). It's an easy wrack to identify. Simply take a short piece off the
end of a frond, hold it towards the
sky, and you will at once see it has a
saw-like edge – hence the popular
name, saw wrack. Generally speaking, it grows from half tide level to
extreme low spring tide level, and
on average is exposed up to half the
time.

Bladder wrack is less fussy about
where it lives. On some shores, it
replaces knotted wrack, while on
others it mingles with it. Sometimes
it is found between knotted and
spiral wrack. Nobody seems to under-
stand the reason for this, so here is
another of those problems remaining

to be solved.

Lastly, as you walk down the
shore, you will come to the sea, and
here grow the tangles and oarweed
(Laminariaceae). To see these at
their best, you will need to visit the
shore on the lowest of spring tides.
There, in the deepest pools, you will
see the great seaweeds growing, a
few with their fronds showing above
the surface. Some will be draped
upon the rocks, glistening in the light.

## Identification of seaweeds

The wracks have quite an easily
recognizable form, as do the larger
laminaria, and one or two others
such as sea oak (Halidrys siliquosa)

41

with its pod-like air bladders, and coral weed (*Corallina officinalis*) with its short, rose-pink fronds.

On the other hand, so many species are alike that even the experts find difficulty in identifying them. But there are many you can try to identify, and by so doing, you will find it easier to tackle the more difficult ones later on.

Knotted wrack is unmistakeable, because its fronds are usually at least 1 metre in length, although in very sheltered areas, it may exceed 3 metres. It has egg-shaped bladders at least the size of the end joint of your thumb. Where conditions suit it, knotted wrack grows in dense masses, and as the tide rises, its long fronds float densely on the water surface and completely obscure the rocks below.

If you examine a plant of knotted wrack, you will find another seaweed which grows on its fronds. It is called tandy (*Polysiphonia lanosa*) and its brownish outline is plain to see. Its holdfast grows into the stem of the host plant, but it obtains its food from the surrounding water. This way of living is termed semi-parasitic. It simply uses knotted wrack as anchorage and living space in an overcrowded environment.

Among the rich variety of seaweeds to be seen in the deepest pools and the sea, is sea belt (*Laminaria saccharina*) which grows up to 3 metres in length. You might like to collect two or three pieces and take them home to use as a weather fore-caster. Fix a piece of strong cord around the holdfast and hang the plant under a porch or on an outside wall. If you want to know what the weather is going to be like, you simply feel the fronds. If they are crisp and dry, it's going to be fine, if they are soft and rubbery, it's going to rain.

It's reasonably reliable because the salt in the plant absorbs moisture from the air, so that when the air is damp before rain, then the plant also becomes damp.

This plant is one of the laminarias that tends to be exposed to the air on

Serrated or saw wrack (*left*) and bladder wrack (*right*).

low spring tides. You will often see the fronds hanging down the sloping face of a rock, so that the entire rock is covered by their frilly fronds.

There is another seaweed somewhat similar to sea belt which is called dabberlocks (*Alaria esculenta*). It tends to grow in places exposed to strong wave action, whereas sea belt favours more sheltered situations. An obvious visual difference is that dabberlocks has a mid-rib along its frond, and its frond is only slightly frilled, whereas sea belt has no mid-rib and its frond is extremely frilled.

A quite spectacular seaweed found in this zone (although it is not a laminaria) is sea bootlaces (*Chorda filum*). You will see it floating on the

sea like lengths of greenish-brown cord about 5 millimetres thick and 4 metres long. It's an annual which is seen at its best in the summer months before it dies off in the winter.

A seaweed which is sometimes confused with it, is sea-thong (*Himanthalia elongata*). On closer inspection you will see one very obvious difference between the two. The individual fronds of sea-thong are split into branches.

When you find some of this seaweed, examine the rock surface nearby, and you will probably find the button-like growths of the young plants, together with even younger plants looking like tiny green mushrooms. If you look at the fully grown plant in early summer, you will see it is covered with tiny spots. These are the reproductive parts, which ripen at that time of the year.

Two large seaweeds that look rather alike, are oarweed (*Laminaria digitata*) and cuvie (*Laminaria hyperborea*). You will find both of these species sticking up out of the water below extreme low spring tide level. They have fronds with a similar branching pattern, like a many fingered hand, with thick stems (stipes) up to 4 centimetres wide. The stem of cuvie is round in cross section, and its holdfast 'rootlets' are short and thick, and bent down sharply towards the rock surface, whereas the stem of tangle is oval, and the holdfast 'rootlets' are thinner and more spread out.

One of the giants among seaweeds is furbelows (*Saccorhiza polyschides*) which in ideal conditions, will grow up to more than 4 metres in length with fronds spreading as wide as 3 metres. Whilst its 'finger-like' fronds could be confused with cuvie and tangle, its stem (stipe) is quite unmistakeable. It is full of curved frills and ends in a thick, rounded, hollow holdfast covered in tiny knobs.

It is a little surprising to learn that this very large seaweed is an annual and can grow its entire bulk in a single year. This ability to grow fast, helps in the survival of any seaweed that grows in places exposed to storms and wave action, and which, in consequence, is frequently broken off or damaged.

In rock pools from half tide level downwards grows a small tufted seaweed that is certain to attract your attention. You will see it sticking out from the sides of pools, and sometimes covering the entire area with its pale mauve fronds. Touch it, and you will find it moves stiffly, and feels hard. It is called coral weed (*Corallina* spp).

Looked at more closely with a hand lens, its unusual structure is revealed. The entire plant is made up of tiny segments, which are covered in a hard deposit of lime. It moves stiffly because only the joints between these segments are free of deposit. When pieces are broken off and die, they become bleached pure white, giving them an almost skele-ton-like appearance.

In the summer, you may come across a small seaweed called oyster thief (*Colpomenia peregrina*). Shaped like a tiny, plum-sized balloon, it is hollow, and when exposed at low tide, often becomes filled with air. Then, when the tide rises, it floats on the surface.

It grows attached by a tiny hold-fast to a variety of other seaweeds, and a local name of bubble-weed is a very apt description of it.

A seaweed which always attracts the eye with its glowing frond ends is carragheen or Irish moss (*Chondrus crispus*). It is purple-red in colour, and glistens in the rock pools with a delightful purple sheen. Unfortunately, if you lift it out of water, this glowing beauty disappears. To see it at its very best, you need to move it gently to and fro in the water, so that parts of it catch the light.

Another which has a beautiful colour underwater, is *Cystoseira tamariscifolia*. It is a shrub-like plant which glows all over with a blue and green iridescence, but remove it from the water, and its lovely colour is immediately lost. There is no mistaking it once you have seen it.

Whilst mentioning attractive and colourful seaweeds, peacock's tail (*Padina pavonia*) should be included. It is a small plant, from 5 to 10 centimetres tall. Its fronds are fan-shaped, stiff and marked with con-centric rings of green, brown and white, the latter colouration being due to a thin coating of lime. If you

*Cystoseira* is a brown seaweed which glows with a blue-green iridescence when seen in a rock pool. It is found at low tide level in the deeper rock pools.

see a collection of small seaweed 'fans', you will recognize them at once as peacock's tail.

On some shores, many rock pools, and even stones within the pools, look as if they have been painted with a thick pink or reddish-violet paint. Even on closer examination, the colour seems almost to be part of the rock itself. It is in fact one of a number of encrusting red seaweeds (*Lithophyllum* or *Lithothamnion* spp).

Their fronds have absorbed calcium and magnesium from the sea, and become quite hard and very,

very thin. Their colour is due to the effect of this calcium on the normal red seaweed. If you see similar patches, but of a white colour, you may well be looking at some dead specimens of the same species which have lost their colour.

Recognizable by its shape, is the pod weed (*Halidrys siliquosa*), known as sea oak. It looks just as if it is covered with small pea pods. They are really air bladders which can vary in length from a few millimetres to nearly 5 centimetres.

I have left until last one of the

easiest of seaweeds to recognize. Its thin, semi-translucent fronds look rather like pieces of irregularly-shaped polythene sheet. If you pick a piece up and stretch it flat between your hands, you can just about see through it. It is called sea-lettuce (*Ulva lactuca*) and its frond may grow to 50 centimetres in length. It will be seen in rock pools attached to small stones on pebbly areas of rocky shores. Here it drapes itself over stones when the tide goes out, and dries out so close to them, that it is like a painted film. Dead specimens, common on the shore, turn to a clear white colour.

## Making a seaweed collection

Many of the smaller seaweeds are very attractive, and can be made into a collection by mounting them on thick paper or card. Wash the specimens thoroughly to remove any surface deposits, and place them into a basin of water. A flat baking dish full of water is ideal, because it allows room for the plant to take up its natural shape. Having done this, you may notice that the plant is too bushy, and that one frond covers another. Cut away some of these fronds whilst still preserving the original shape of the outline. The specimen is then ready to mount.

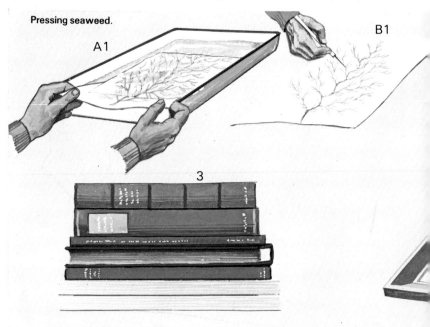

Pressing seaweed.

A1

B1

3

The actual mounting can be done in either of two ways. Both require moderately thick, plain drawing paper, cut to a size sufficiently large to allow a small space all around the specimen when it is in place.

Having cut the paper, the first method of mounting seaweed is to slip the paper into the water beneath the plant, and then, very slowly, lift it up under the plant and out of the water (method A1). With practice and with the aid of a small paint brush to steer wayward pieces into position, you will finish up with your specimen in close contact with the paper. It is a method recommended in many books, but it is extremely tricky to do. The main problem is that the paper can become so saturated, that it wrinkles up.

A much easier method is as follows. Cut the paper as before and lay it on a flat surface. Take a very careful look at the natural outline and shape of your specimen in the dish. Next, lift it out and drop it on to the paper. It will be thoroughly wet so you will be able to arrange the fronds in their natural positions with a paint brush (method B1). If some of the fronds tend to stick to the paper, drop a little water on to them before easing them into position.

As soon as the seaweed is arranged, try to mop up excess moisture on a brush or small piece of blotting paper. Do not under any circumstances place blotting paper entirely over the specimen – it will stick to it!

Now lay the paper on a thick pad of old newspapers until nearly dry. When nearly dry, flatten the paper out and cover it with greaseproof paper (2) and a book, piece of wood, or any flat heavy object to press the seaweed flat (3). Your next mounted specimen can then be placed on top of this, and so on, repeating the process.

When thoroughly dry and pressed, the seaweed pages can be formed into a book, or even mounted on card or hardboard as pictures (4). However, if exposed to daylight for any length of time, seaweeds lose their colour and become that much less attractive.

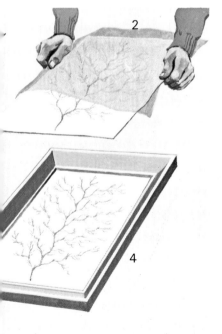

Here is a selection of plants and animals
that live on rocky shores.

# Anemones

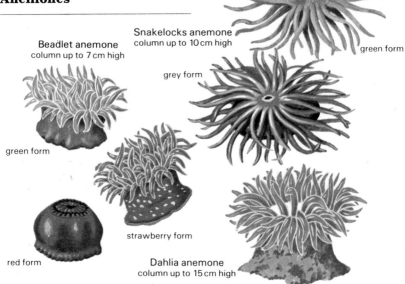

Beadlet anemone
column up to 7 cm high

Snakelocks anemone
column up to 10 cm high

green form

grey form

green form

strawberry form

red form

Dahlia anemone
column up to 15 cm high

# Tube worms

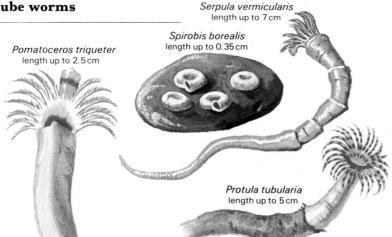

*Serpula vermicularis*
length up to 7 cm

*Spirobis borealis*
length up to 0.35 cm

*Pomatoceros triqueter*
length up to 2.5 cm

*Protula tubularia*
length up to 5 cm

# Barnacles

### Star barnacle
shell up to 1.2 cm in diameter

### Acorn barnacle
shell up to 1.5 cm in diameter

# Molluscs

### Common limpet
shell up to 7 cm long

### Flat periwinkle
shell up to 1 cm high

### Rough periwinkle
shell up to 0.8 cm high

### Edible periwinkle
shell up to 2.5 cm high

### Small periwinkle
shell up to 0.5 cm high

### Thick top-shell
shell up to 2.5 cm high

### Grey top-shell
shell up to 1.25 cm high

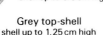

hermit crab
in shell

### Purple top-shell
shell up to 1.25 cm high

### Painted top-shell
shell up to 2.5 cm high

### European cowrie
shell up to 1.2 cm long

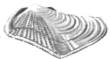

### Oval piddock
shell up to 9 cm long

### Paper piddock
shell up to 5.5 cm long

### Little piddock
shell up to 5 cm long

# Crabs and lobsters

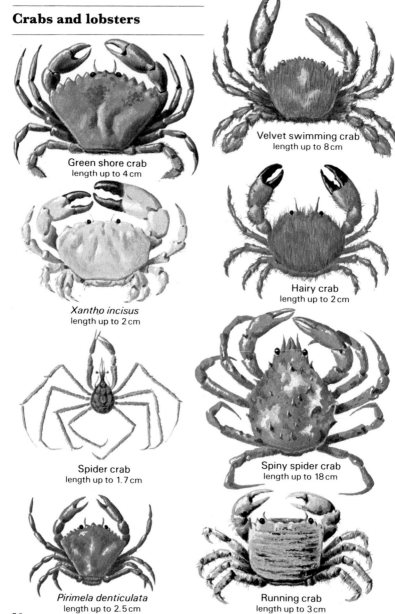

Green shore crab
length up to 4 cm

Velvet swimming crab
length up to 8 cm

*Xantho incisus*
length up to 2 cm

Hairy crab
length up to 2 cm

Spider crab
length up to 1.7 cm

Spiny spider crab
length up to 18 cm

*Pirimela denticulata*
length up to 2.5 cm

Running crab
length up to 3 cm

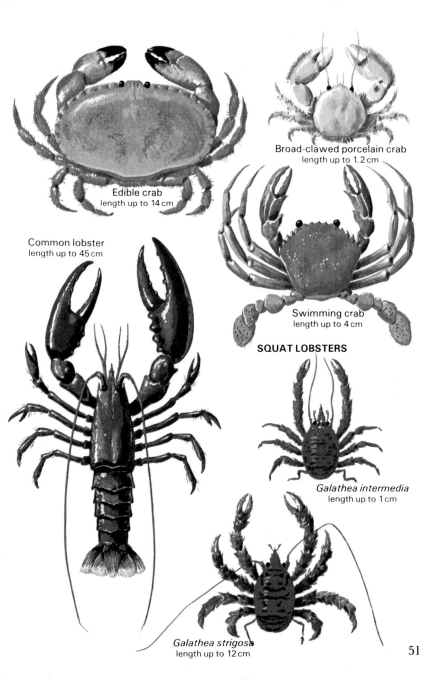

Edible crab
length up to 14 cm

Broad-clawed porcelain crab
length up to 1.2 cm

Common lobster
length up to 45 cm

Swimming crab
length up to 4 cm

**SQUAT LOBSTERS**

*Galathea intermedia*
length up to 1 cm

*Galathea strigosa*
length up to 12 cm

51

# Fish of the shore

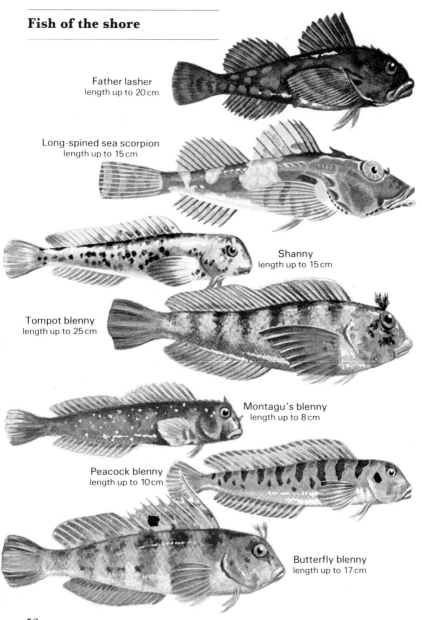

Father lasher
length up to 20 cm

Long-spined sea scorpion
length up to 15 cm

Shanny
length up to 15 cm

Tompot blenny
length up to 25 cm

Montagu's blenny
length up to 8 cm

Peacock blenny
length up to 10 cm

Butterfly blenny
length up to 17 cm

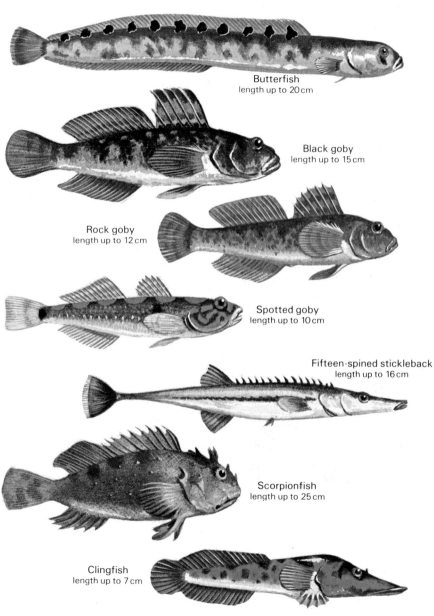

Butterfish
length up to 20 cm

Black goby
length up to 15 cm

Rock goby
length up to 12 cm

Spotted goby
length up to 10 cm

Fifteen-spined stickleback
length up to 16 cm

Scorpionfish
length up to 25 cm

Clingfish
length up to 7 cm

53

# Sponges and sea-squirts

Purse sponge
growths up to 5 cm long

Breadcrumb sponge
growths up to 20 cm across

Sulphur sponge
growths up to 30 cm in diameter

*Sycon ciliatum* (sponge)
growths up to 3 cm high

*Hymeniacidon sanguinea* (sponge)
growths up to 50 cm wide

*Ciona intestinalis*
height up to 17 cm

**SEA SQUIRTS**

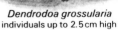

Star ascidian
individuals up to 0.3 cm long

*Phallusia mammillata*
individuals up to 20 cm long

*Ascidia mentula*
height up to 10 cm

*Dendrodoa grossularia*
individuals up to 2.5 cm high

54

# Sea urchins and starfish

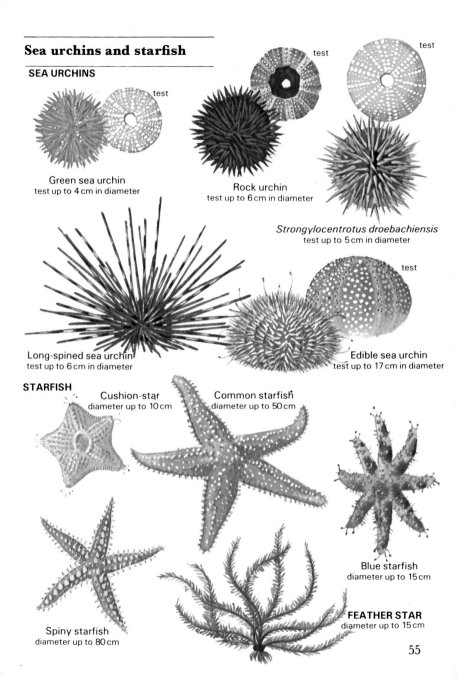

## SEA URCHINS

Green sea urchin
test up to 4 cm in diameter

Rock urchin
test up to 6 cm in diameter

*Strongylocentrotus droebachiensis*
test up to 5 cm in diameter

Long-spined sea urchin
test up to 6 cm in diameter

Edible sea urchin
test up to 17 cm in diameter

## STARFISH

Cushion-star
diameter up to 10 cm

Common starfish
diameter up to 50 cm

Blue starfish
diameter up to 15 cm

Spiny starfish
diameter up to 80 cm

**FEATHER STAR**
diameter up to 15 cm

# Seaweeds

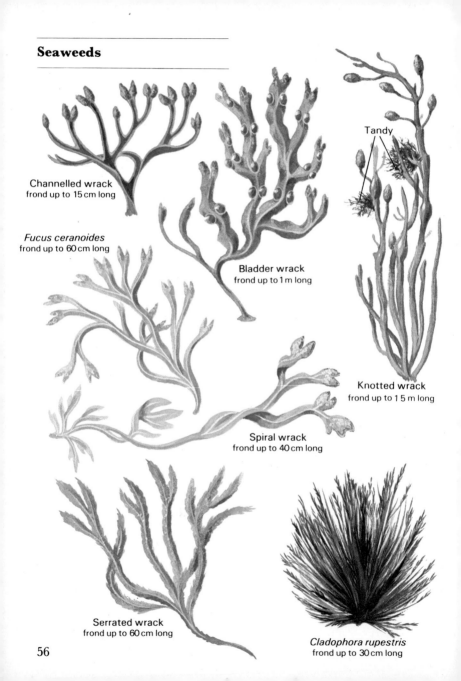

Channelled wrack
frond up to 15 cm long

*Fucus ceranoides*
frond up to 60 cm long

Bladder wrack
frond up to 1 m long

Tandy

Knotted wrack
frond up to 1 5 m long

Spiral wrack
frond up to 40 cm long

Serrated wrack
frond up to 60 cm long

*Cladophora rupestris*
frond up to 30 cm long

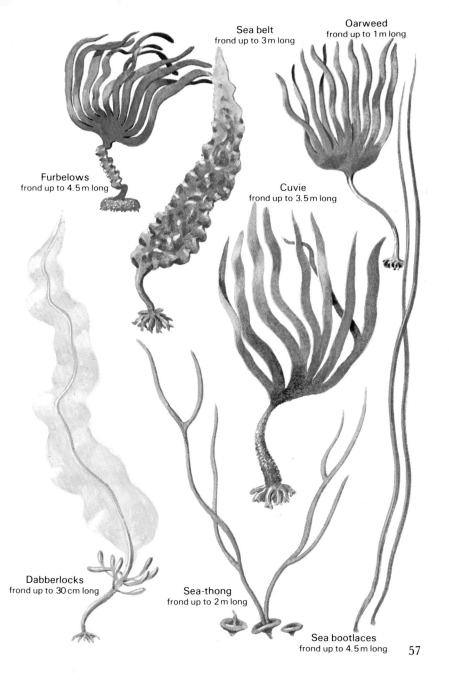

Sea belt
frond up to 3 m long

Oarweed
frond up to 1 m long

Furbelows
frond up to 4.5 m long

Cuvie
frond up to 3.5 m long

Dabberlocks
frond up to 30 cm long

Sea-thong
frond up to 2 m long

Sea bootlaces
frond up to 4.5 m long

57

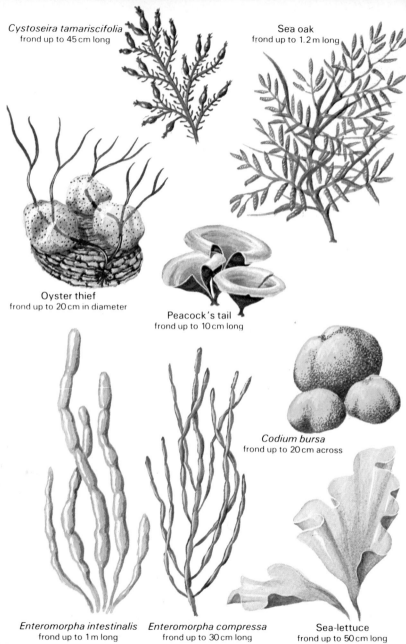

*Cystoseira tamariscifolia*
frond up to 45 cm long

Sea oak
frond up to 1.2 m long

Oyster thief
frond up to 20 cm in diameter

Peacock's tail
frond up to 10 cm long

*Codium bursa*
frond up to 20 cm across

*Enteromorpha intestinalis*
frond up to 1 m long

*Enteromorpha compressa*
frond up to 30 cm long

Sea-lettuce
frond up to 50 cm long

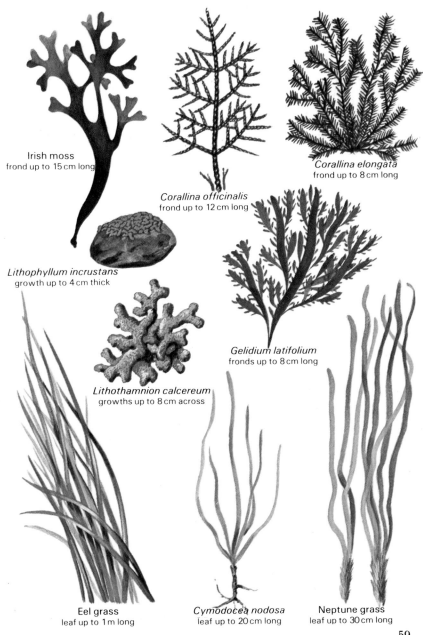

Irish moss
frond up to 15 cm long

*Corallina officinalis*
frond up to 12 cm long

*Corallina elongata*
frond up to 8 cm long

*Lithophyllum incrustans*
growth up to 4 cm thick

*Gelidium latifolium*
fronds up to 8 cm long

*Lithothamnion calcereum*
growths up to 8 cm across

Eel grass
leaf up to 1 m long

*Cymodocea nodosa*
leaf up to 20 cm long

Neptune grass
leaf up to 30 cm long

# Sandy shores

On a sandy beach in midsummer, thousands of people walk and run across the sand, yet very few of them realize the vast amount of life a few centimetres below their feet. There is a whole world beneath the sand where animals hunt their prey, find protection from surface enemies, or live quiet sedentary lives.

If you think for a moment about the nature of sand, you will begin to realize some of the problems involved in living in it. Firstly, there is no possibility of a firm foothold upon its surface, nor are there any solid areas on which seaweeds can find attachment. So naturally, you will not expect to find many of the rocky

A desert-like strip of sandy beach can hide a host of animals living beneath it. Buried by sand, and living in burrows, they reveal their presence by small holes, raised mounds and tracks and signs of many kinds.

shore animals living in – what is to them – a hostile environment.

On the rocky shore, animals can find protection in crevices and beneath rocks. They can survive by clinging and gripping in a wide variety of ways. Sucker discs, claws, large flat crawling feet and animal 'cement' all help the creatures.

But none of these adaptations are much good on the sandy beach. To survive there, an animal must either swim over it or burrow down into it. Indeed, the vast majority of life there depends upon its ability to burrow.

Burrowing into the moist sand has an added advantage when the tide goes out, because the animal is safe from drying winds and hot sun. It is essential for the animals to avoid drying out, and in the absence of damp rock crevices and the shelter of seaweed curtains, there is no other alternative to burrowing.

## The nature of sand

If you take a sample of sand and examine it with a hand lens, you will discover a number of facts about it. Generally speaking, it is composed of very tiny grains, and most of these started either as cliffs, or were deposited on the beach by rivers.

A close look at the grains reveals that a large percentage of them are the same colour, and indeed of the same material as nearby cliffs. Over millions of years, waves have pounded the cliffs, rain water has soaked in, frozen and split them, and large masses have thus broken off and fallen into the sea.

Here the waves have worked on them by rolling them about, bombarding them with sand grains and pebbles, and generally acting like a vast hammer. So the rock mass became a boulder, the boulder a rock, then a pebble and finally a sand grain.

Due to the immense power of the sea, a great deal of the sand is also carried from some distance away. This accounts for some of the other coloured grains.

As you look through the hand lens, you will see many tiny flattish particles that are the broken-down remains of shells. The amount of these in any sample of sand depends upon many factors such as exposure of the beach to wave action, and nearness of a rocky area providing a large population of molluscs.

If you look really closely at a sample of sand, you will see spaces between the grains. Normally, these will be filled with seawater, and even when the tide is out, the sand, especially on the lower parts of the shore, remains waterlogged. This water in the sand provides oxygen for the animals to breathe, and moisture to prevent them drying out.

## Worms in the sand

By their very shape, worms are perfectly suited to living in sand, and there are several species.

### Sand mason worm

Search along the lower margins of a beach, and you will come upon small sandy tubes sticking up out of the sand. Some of them will have branched tops rather like miniature palm trees, and the actual tubes will be about the same thickness as a pencil. These are the structures made by sand mason worms (*Lanice conchilega*), which go down over 50 centimetres. Within a tube, the delicate body of the sand mason is well protected. The worm has many long tentacles at its head end, and when building the tube, it uses these to probe among the sand and gather up suitably sized pieces. Each piece is then drawn in to the tube end where it is cemented into place by a fluid secreted from glands on the underside of the worm's body. The building work is done by the mouth.

*Above*: The branched tops of sand mason worms. *Below*: The worms and their tubes.

Sometimes, due to rough seas or the pressure of human feet, the top of the tube is broken off. Soon after this happens, the sand mason begins to rebuild, and in a matter of a few hours, its tube is restored.

From the top rim of the tube extend a number of short threads, each made from tiny pieces of shell or sand cemented one to another. These open outwards to form an improvised funnel, and this serves to trap drifting particles of food which the worm then eats. However, its main method of feeding is to use its tentacles to gather fragments of plant and animal debris from the sand surface.

You can collect these worms by digging deeply with a fork. Push it in a few centimetres from one of the tubes, and make sure you push it *straight* down, otherwise you may cut across the tube and damage the worm. Dig at least 30 centimetres down – deeper if possible. The tube should come up near the centre of the forkful of sand and it must be handled with great care, for it will break very easily. Gently separate it from the sand and put it in a bucket with a little seawater.

Since these worms are quick to sense disturbance of any kind, most of your tubes will be empty. The worms will have shot out of the end. Therefore, you need to collect several tubes to be sure of having one or two live specimens.

If you put these in an aquarium tank, you will be able to watch them build. Simply place a layer of sand about 1 centimetre deep on the bottom of the tank and put the tubeworms on this. Then cover them with about 3 centimetres depth of sand.

If you already have a sub-sand filter covered by sand (see the chapter on marine aquariums) place the two layers on top of the sand or gravel already covering the filter.

## Lugworm

Most sandy or muddy beaches have the distinctive signs of the lugworm (*Arenicola marina*), in quantity. You will probably be familiar with those coiled sandy 'worms' and small saucer-like depressions on the beach. They indicate that under the sand is a lugworm's burrow.

It is U-shaped and the lugworm lines it with mucus. In this way, it forms a burrow which does not collapse. The lugworm lives in the bottom curve of the burrow between 20 and 30 centimetres below the sand surface.

When feeding, the lugworm swallows mouthfuls of sand which 'fall' down from the saucer shaped depression. From this sand, it takes anything edible, like seaweed fragments and pieces of animal matter, but in order to satisfy its hunger, it has to swallow large quantities of sand. In this process, the inedible sand is ejected and is thrown up on the surface, to form the familiar worm cast.

A big lugworm can be as thick as your little finger, and up to 20 centimetres long. When handled, it discharges a yellowish-brown fluid

In the process of building their burrows and feeding, lugworms eject these wormlike mounds of sand. Usually a 'blow hole' is to be seen nearby.

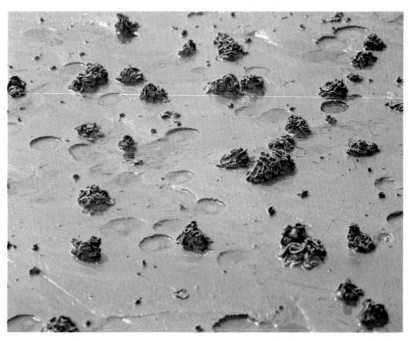

which stains your hands, but it's not too messy, so you might like to dig one up.

Dig down about 10 to 15 centimetres parallel to an imaginary line joining a cast and blowhole. If you place the worm on some wet sand, you will be able to see how it burrows by pushing its proboscis (an elongated feeding organ) into the sand. Ripples then spread along its body, and help it to move quickly under the sand.

### Catworm

As you dig on the beach, you will almost certainly come across a catworm (*Nephthys hombergi*). It's a pinky-whitish coloured worm which can grow to 20 centimetres in length, although the average size is nearer 10 centimetres. No sooner is it exposed than it immediately begins to burrow down into the sand again, and the speed with which it disappears is truly amazing.

## Shell-life

A rich variety of shells is to be found living beneath the sand, but the only signs of their presence are small holes of various shapes, and a few empty shells left by the receding tide. If a shell is to survive on a sandy shore, it must be adapted to a burrowing way of life. Since sand is a fairly 'solid' medium to move through, the less resistance offered by the shell valves, the easier it is to move downwards.

In consequence, nearly all the shell-life of sandy shores are bivalves (animals with shells in two parts hinged together). Their shell valves are flattened and they have extra large feet for digging, displacing sand, or pushing themselves over flat soft surfaces. Because they live actually buried in and surrounded by sand, breathing would be a problem, but sand dwelling molluscs have overcome this difficulty by developing extra long syphon tubes which they extend upwards above the sand surface. One of these syphons draws in seawater from which the animal takes in oxygen. The water is circulated through the mollusc, and is then passed out through the other syphon.

Unlike the molluscs of a rocky shore which actively move about in search of food, the sandy shore species have to use what is available close by. Instead of going after food, they have to wait for the food to come to them, and the sea, with its daily changing tides and currents, does this very effectively, by bringing in a new supply of food twice a day.

It comes in the form of drifting plankton, or is left on the sand by the waves. The buried molluscs either push up their syphons and draw down the plankton and filter it out, or use them to probe about the sand surface for particles of food. The latter method is rather like the long tube of a vacuum cleaner sucking up pieces off the carpet.

## Razor shells

The long, narrow shell valves of the razor shells (Solenidae) are quite unmistakeable and the living molluscs are fantastic burrowers and can burrow down faster than anyone can dig. They have a speed of descent of up to half a metre in three seconds.

To find a living razor shell, you will first have to search for its signs. Choose a day with a low spring tide and walk slowly *backwards* along the sand. As you do so, look down at the sand between your feet, and if a razor shell is there, you will see a sudden jet of water shoot into the air. As it subsides, you will see a hole appear in the sand, which opens rapidly as the water left in it drains away.

What actually happens is that the razor shell, lying a few centimetres under the sand, feels the vibration from your feet, and immediately retreats downwards. The jet of water is the result of this sudden reaction.

Its method of burrowing shows how well some animals have adapted to this way of life. To begin the action, it pushes its long foot out from the lower end of the shell valves, downwards through the sand for about 5 to 7 centimetres. Next it pumps blood into its foot, which swells into a small bulb, and so helps it to secure a grip. Powerful muscles then pull the shell valves down on to this swollen foot. The action is repeated quickly, so the razor shell

'dives' down in a series of jerks, which in fact, are so smooth that they appear to be a single movement.

If you prefer to simply search for the syphon holes in the sand, you will soon learn to recognize their distinctive shape and size.

There is no simple trick to digging a razor shell out. It's rather a question of how hard you are prepared to

work. Push your spade in at least 12 centimetres from the hole, for if you go too close, you will break the mollusc in half.

Because they are so good to eat and so difficult to catch, fishermen on some beaches have invented a spearing technique. They make a metre-long spear from 5 millimetre thick wire, iron or steel rod, with a

Colourful shells of many kinds are to be found on the tide line. Many have parts worn away by wave and sand action. *Inset*: This razor shell is alive and will soon rebury itself.

small spearhead barb at one end and a handle at the other. They then push the spear down into the hole, feeling for the razor shell which, when detected, is hauled out on the barb.

*Above*: Red-nose cockles disturbed from their burrows showing their large red feet.

*Below*: A cockle leaping on its muscular foot.

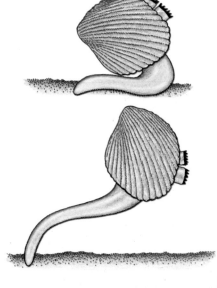

### Wedge shells

The most attractive of all are the wedge shells (Donacidae) with their infinite variety of colours. The banded wedge shell (*Donax vittatus*) can be off-white, yellow, brown or violet with the interior of the shell white or violet, and it is very highly polished. The collection of these shells will provide hours of searching, for on those beaches where they are well established, there are many to be found.

### Cockles

These are quite common on some sandy shores. Generally, they live below the tide levels, but are sometimes to be found near the limit of low spring tides. The giant red-nose or spiny cockle (*Acanthocardia aculeata*) grows to over 8 centimetres long. It has a large red foot and orange body-fringe to the shell. The cockle is the gymnast among the shell animals. If it is stranded on the beach, or attacked by a predator, it will somersault away. It does this by extending its long red foot, pressing the tip into the sand and thrusting its body over in an arc. When you find a spiny cockle or a common cockle (see page 97) see if you can spot the growth rings that run around the shell valves. Unfortunately, they give only an approximate idea of the age of the shell, but you will probably notice that some of the shells have one or more deeply ridged ring. This is a sign that the cockle has undergone some sort of disturbance such as being washed out of the sand by a storm, and it is known as a disturbance ring.

## Mussels

These creatures anchor themselves by special threads called byssus threads which are secreted by the foot and attached to rocks, pier piles and similar objects. Mussels (*Mytilus* spp) feed by drawing in seawater and filtering out the thousands of tiny floating particles. Some idea of their rate of filtering can be gained from the fact that an average size mussel filters every particle from 45 litres of seawater every 24 hours.

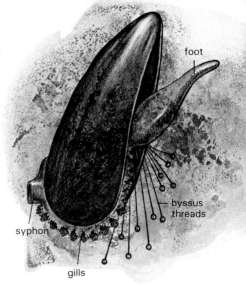

A mussel survives storms because it is anchored by elastic threads.

## Queen scallop

Most of the creatures that live in seashells can see quite well, for they have eyes. The queen scallop (*Chlamys opercularis*) has two rows of eyes, each with a focussing lens, rather like our own.

This creature is jet-propelled, and its method of swimming is rather interesting. It is a bivalve and therefore has two valves to its shell. A little way inside these valves are two fleshy curtains. One hangs down from the upper shell valve, and the other projects upwards from the lower valve. When the queen wants to swim, it opens its valves quite wide, and water flows in. Next, it snaps shut the valves, and the two 'curtains' prevent the water escaping

A scallop swims by opening its shells, taking in water then shooting it out through a jet.

from the front. Under pressure from the closing valves, the water is pushed out through holes at the hinge end, or back, and so the queen is jet propelled forward. At the same time, a small quantity of water is pushed outwards and downwards, and this helps to keep the queen from sinking. A series of such movements enables it to swim quite long distances, and each jet 'push' may send it 30 centimetres through the water.

The fact that queen scallops can cover considerable distances is certain, for it is known that they migrate. They are not found in the same place throughout the year, but how far they go and their actual migration routes are still not known.

### Canoe shell

One of the most fantastic swimmers is the canoe shell (*Akera bullata*). The body of this creature has developed two flaps, which it uses as wings to 'fly' through the water when escaping from a predator. It is a very beautiful sight as it swims, for it spins slowly, and rises and falls in 'flight'.

### Violet sea snail

The violet sea snail (*Ianthina exigua*), has a very thin and light shell, and it secretes a bubble-filled float from which it hangs down and drifts through the seas. Blown by the winds from warmer areas of the Atlantic it is an occasional visitor to north European waters. It has the unusual habit of feeding on a small jellyfish (*Velella velella*) called by-the-wind-sailor because it has a small sail-like

A violet sea snail makes its own bubble raft and floats on the sea surface.

flap on its top surface which catches the wind.

## Other shells you may find

Holes of differing shapes and small humps in the sand, are usually the signs of buried shells. A little gentle digging and careful sorting of the sand will uncover the animal.

Trough shells (Mactridae), tellins (Tellinidae), Venus shells (Veneridae) and sunset shells (Asaphidae) will all be found on sandy shores. Many of these molluscs with their flat shells, are ideally suited to moving through the sand in search of fresh feeding areas. Their shells are very beautiful, with delicate colours and many have deep grooves.

---

## Hunters in the sand

---

With so many shells crowding the beach, it is not surprising that there are predators which have become very efficient at hunting them.

### Necklace shells

There are several species of these predators known broadly as sea snails, necklace shells or natica (Naticidae). Their shells are glossy, and shaped like a typical garden snail. A necklace shell has an enormous foot which, when inflated with sea water, is very much larger than its shell.

Forcing its way through the sand, it explores for any bivalve mollusc it can find and as soon as it comes in contact, it wraps its prey in its foot. On the underside of its proboscis is a small disc-shaped gland which gives off an acid which helps to dissolve the shell of its prey. A small hole is thus formed, and through this, the necklace shell feeds on the living body of its prey.

### Dogwhelk

Another hunter, the common dogwhelk (*Nucella lapillus*) preys in a similar way upon barnacles and mussels. It has a tongue which bores a small hole in the shell of its prey and to help enlarge this hole, it secretes an acid which actually softens it. As soon as the tiny 2 millimetre hole is complete, the dogwhelk inserts its proboscis.

### Burrowing starfish

Another hungry hunter is the burrowing starfish (*Astropecten irregularis*) which occasionally hunts over the sand surface, but more often burrows down and then moves through the sand. Its prey consists of small crabs, shellfish and worms. These it swallows whole through its mouth which is placed at the central meeting point of its five arms.

If you are able to find one, and at the same time collect a common starfish (*Asterias* spp) from a rocky shore, it is interesting to compare them. Both have five arms and perhaps at first glance, look a little alike. But if you look closely at the massed feet on the undersides, you will see one great difference. The common starfish has tube feet which end in small suckers. These help it to cling to the rocks on which it lives and also to grip and open *large* shells to feed. The burrowing starfish has tube feet which end in a point and are ideal for burrowing. As it swallows *small* prey whole, it has no need to open them.

So here you have two animals almost alike, yet each adapted to a different habitat.

Arms of different starfish

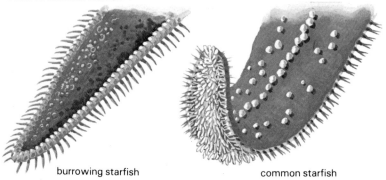

burrowing starfish                          common starfish

*Below*: Burrowing starfish in the process of reburying themselves in the sand.

# Sand-dwelling sea urchins

The sea potato (*Echinocardium cordatum*) is to be found near low tide and the sign to look for is an irregular hole less than 1 centimetre across, and often rather star-shaped. Being related to starfish, sea potatoes have tube feet, and their very delicate bodies are covered in golden spines. These spines are of great interest, as you will discover if you dig up a specimen (which you can easily do with your hand).

Look at the underside of the animal, and you will see the mouth slit and nearby, a group of many spoon-shaped spines. You will see waves of movement passing across them, and these spines are the main ones that are used for burrowing. The spines slowly push the sand grains out of the way, and this you can see for yourself by placing a sea potato back on to the surface of wet sand. Within a very short time, you will see sand building up around the edge of the urchin as it slowly sinks down. Once settled in its burrow, the urchin builds a narrow shaft to the surface and down this a current of water is drawn for breathing purposes. The shaft is kept open by a lining of mucus, and the action of long tube feet. Another shaft is made horizontally behind the urchin to contain all excreted waste, and the burrow is therefore kept clean.

As you walk along a beach where these urchins live, you may well see a freshly opened one, split in two. How it comes to be at the surface to allow this to happen is a mystery, but the culprit that has eaten it is undoubtedly a herring gull.

# Life in sandy pools and shallows

Whilst most of the species already described will also be found in sandy pools and shallows, there are a few different ones to look for too.

### Lesser weever

Let's start with a rather unpleasant fish, about 12 centimetres long, called the lesser weever (*Trachinus vipera*). It spends much of its time buried in the sand and remains like that, with just its eyes uncovered, waiting for shrimps and smaller fish to come close.

But the dangerous part of the weever is its dorsal fin. The rear end of this fin is coloured black and armed with sharp grooved spines which are connected to small poison sacs. When frightened, it erects these, and if you are unfortunate enough to step on it, a very painful wound results.

Considering how comparatively common this species is on some beaches, it is surprising that so few bathers ever get 'stung'. It is possible that the large number of holiday-makers playing around in the water, drives the weevers out into deeper water, where people swim over them.

If you go shrimping, it's a good plan to wear some sort of footwear to guard against this fish. Remember too, to search carefully in a shrimp net and do not attempt to pick up one of these fish. They really are dangerous. Should you be so unfortunate as to be 'stung' by a weever, go and receive medical attention as quickly as possible.

### Daisy anemone

This sea anemone has successfully settled on soft sand. The daisy anemone (*Cereus pedunculatus*) has a disc which is usually attached to a buried stone, 12 centimetres or more below the surface, and all that can be seen of it is the circle of short, brown and cream tentacles spread over the sand. A careful search in sandy pools near low tide may reveal one or more of these.

### Shrimps

At first glance a sandy pool seems to be totally devoid of life, but if you begin to look very closely, you may see the slightest movement of a buried shrimp (*Crangon crangon*).

It's a beautifully camouflaged little animal, brown or grey with reddish dots. Even when walking over the sand, it blends so perfectly that only movement gives it away, and during daytime it moves very little, preferring to remain covered with a thin layer of sand. It has many enemies and is eaten by fish of all kinds and also shorebirds.

When you discover a shrimp, catch it and then release it in the pool and watch how quickly it burrows, using its legs to push the sand aside. Within about 20 seconds, it is almost out of sight, and it then uses its long antennae to brush sand

The daisy anemone may be found in muddy sand where it attaches itself to a stone below the sand. In rock pools it pushes its body down into narrow cracks.

74

over any exposed parts. And so it disappears.

Shrimps are good scavengers and take a great variety of foods such as the eggs of a number of marine creatures, small crabs and vegetable matter such as decaying seaweed. Its front nipper claws are strong enough to deal with sand worms longer than itself.

According to the season, you may be fortunate to see a shrimp carrying its load of eggs, which you will see among the swimming appendages on its underside. Local fishermen often refer to shrimps in this condition as 'berried'. They carry their eggs for several weeks, whilst the young develop, and finally the young larvae burst out of the eggs and float up to join the rest of the plankton drifting in the sea. After a short period, during which their numbers rapidly dwindle, the lucky ones settle on to the sand and eventually grow into sizeable shrimps.

When you consider the number of predators preying upon them from the moment they break free of the egg until they become adults and eventually die, it's surprising how plentiful they are.

## Gobies

As a family, the gobies have expanded into a number of different habitats and will be found in both tropical and temperate waters, estuaries, freshwater and around the coasts generally. You will find them in shallow sandy pools as well as in rock pools (see page 30) but, like the shrimp, they are remarkably well camouflaged.

## Flatfish

Sandy pools are a temporary home for a variety of young flatfishes, but you will only discover these if you practise the following technique. Use a small twig or pencil and slowly move it through the top centimetre of sand. Disturb as much of the sand as possible and eventually you may see a tiny flatfish swim away. Watch it as it settles and see how it undulates its body to raise the sand into a sort of mist which then settles on, and covers, its body. I have seen large flatfish use a very special technique to camouflage themselves. They swim a few centimetres above the sand and then plunge down on to it, flapping their tails to send up a great cloud of sand. Then they do a rapid turn, swim back into the cloud, settle on the bottom and let the sand fall on to them.

On emergence from the egg, the larval fish look very much like the early stages of mackerel, bass, mullet and so on, as they do not settle on the bottom nor swim 'flat'.

As they begin to grow into the likeness of small fish, their bodies become increasingly deeper, especially at the front end. It is then that a quiet remarkable change occurs. The bones of the skull actually begin to twist around, and very slowly, over a period of weeks, the eye moves around with it. This can be the left eye or the right according to the species.

Eventually, both eyes are on the same side of the head, and since the body shape has also changed, the young fish has taken to swimming on its side. It is then a flatfish.

### Mullet

In late summer, shoals of baby mullet (Mugilidae) appear, each about 4 centimetres long. They swim close to the surface near the shore, and often you will come across as few as five or six together. No doubt they are survivors from an attack on their shoal.

## Shrimping on the sandy shore

Shrimping is a really delightful pasttime for a sunny summer afternoon. All you need is a shrimp net, which can be bought at a local shop, or if you are particularly keen, you might like to make one yourself. Details are given in the chapter on equipment.

There are basically two reasons for going shrimping, the first to catch yourself a tasty meal, and the second to have a closer look at the rich variety of life that lives in this narrow band of the shallows.

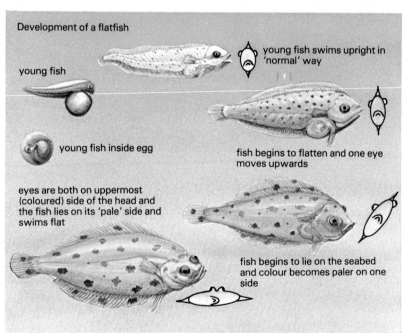

Development of a flatfish

young fish

young fish inside egg

young fish swims upright in 'normal' way

fish begins to flatten and one eye moves upwards

eyes are both on uppermost (coloured) side of the head and the fish lies on its 'pale' side and swims flat

fish begins to lie on the seabed and colour becomes paler on one side

All sorts of sea creatures can be caught with a small net.

If your reason is to discover this life, then you will need a plastic bucket, or better still, a shallow baking dish of some kind. Fill this with water, leave it just beyond the edge of the tide, and wade out until your knees are well covered – slightly deeper water is even better. You will find pushing a large net is quite hard work, but in spite of this, do try to keep it moving steadily, i.e. at a fast walking pace.

Sometimes, as you move along, you will see small fish jump out of the water to avoid the net. It's a good sign that there are plenty about, and it also underlines the reason for walking fast – you are much more likely to net them.

Keep pushing the net as you travel parallel to the shore, and after about 100 metres, turn in a wide circle and return to your starting point. By this time, you should have a reasonable variety of species in your net, so go back to your basin and lay the net down. Usually, it looks as if you had been trawling for seaweed, and I have known times when there was so much that shrimping became impractical. A small amount of seaweed is to be expected, however.

Begin to search gently and carefully by picking up pieces of weed and removing them. Never plunge your fingers in to grasp handfuls, or you might seize a weever. As the seaweed is reduced, every so often you will make a discovery. Pick it up gently and place it in the basin. You can examine it more closely in a minute. Perhaps there will be several shrimps and a flatfish, or a masked crab smothered in clinging sea-lettuce. Disentangle it and put it with your growing collection.

There will most likely be hermit crabs (Paguridae) in a great variety of shells, although these are more common on some beaches than others. In the end, you will have tossed out all the seaweed and rescued all the animals, having returned the unwanted ones to the sea. Do not leave them stranded on the sand.

**Cuttlefish**
Perhaps you will catch a beautiful little animal called the little cuttle (*Sepiola atlantica*) and this really is a good find. About 2 centimetres in length, it is quite common on some sandy shores, but due to its habit of burying in the surface sand, it is not too frequently caught in shrimp nets. Handle this little fellow very gently and watch carefully as you release it in the basin. It may well shoot out a tiny cloud of jet black sepia, which is one of its methods of defence.

If you look closely as it swims about, you will see a tiny tube projecting just below its head. Through this, it forces out water in a jet stream, and this is how it moves so fast. By altering the direction of this jet it can make quite sudden turns, as well as reversing when necessary.

Spread some fine sand to a depth of about 3 centimetres in the bottom of your basin, and you will be able to discover how the little cuttlefish hides itself. Using a combination of its jet directed downwards towards the sand, and the rapid movement of its tiny 'fins', it sinks slowly into the sand. Sometimes it pauses, as if exhausted with the effort, but in much less than a minute, it is nearly buried. To complete its camouflage, it uses its tentacles to draw tiny pebbles and sand over its body, until only the two eyes can be seen, and even these are camouflaged to look like the sand.

Make several trips as there is no end to what you may find. It is up to you whether you return all of your catch to the sea or take some home to study more closely in your aquarium, but never forget, there are always fresh beaches to search.

The little cuttle is smaller than the common cuttlefish, only growing up to 5 centimetres. It swims over or buries itself in sand in shallow water. Once buried, it waits for a small crab or shrimp to approach which it seizes in its tentacles.

Here is a selection of animals that live on sandy shores.

## Worms in the sand

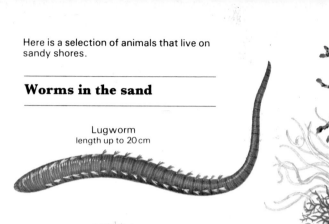

Lugworm
length up to 20 cm

Catworm
length up to 20 cm

tube

worm removed
from tube

Sand mason
length up to 30 cm

## Shell-life

Razor shell
shell up to 12.5 cm long

Pod razor shell
shell up to 20 cm long

Grooved razor shell
shell up to 12.5 cm long

80

**Banded wedge shell**
shell up to 3.75 cm long

**Prickly cockle**
shell up to 7.5 cm long

**Spiny cockle**
shell up to 10 cm long

**Queen scallop**
shell up to 9 cm long

**Canoe shell**
shell up to 4.5 cm long

**Violet sea snail**
shell up to 1.5 cm high

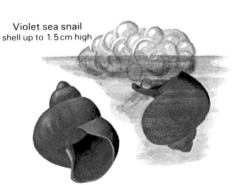

# Hunters in the sand

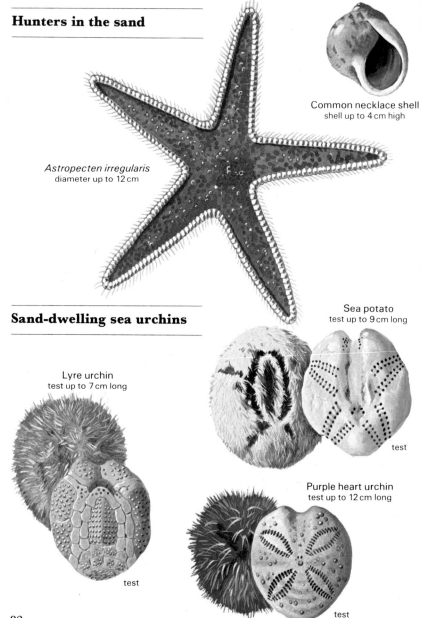

Common necklace shell
shell up to 4 cm high

*Astropecten irregularis*
diameter up to 12 cm

# Sand-dwelling sea urchins

Sea potato
test up to 9 cm long

Lyre urchin
test up to 7 cm long

test

Purple heart urchin
test up to 12 cm long

test

test

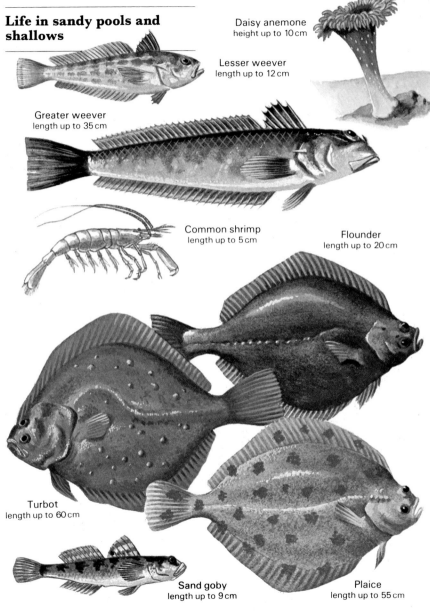

# Life in sandy pools and shallows

Daisy anemone
height up to 10 cm

Lesser weever
length up to 12 cm

Greater weever
length up to 35 cm

Common shrimp
length up to 5 cm

Flounder
length up to 20 cm

Turbot
length up to 60 cm

Sand goby
length up to 9 cm

Plaice
length up to 55 cm

83

# Shingle beaches

Shingle beaches, by their very composition, are inhospitable habitats for animals, although many highly specialized plants have succeeded in colonizing such beaches.

As soon as you walk on to the shingle you will begin to realize the problems. You will find your feet sink into it and slip slightly as you stride forward. You will feel the small stones moving under your feet and if there are waves breaking you will hear the roar of countless pebbles rubbing against each other.

Just try to imagine what it would be like to be a small animal trying to survive there. How could it possibly avoid being crushed by all those whirling stones? In the event of any organisms settling on some of these stones, they would quickly be killed and reduced to dust. It is precisely

Shingle beaches are a difficult habitat for animals and plants. Stones and pebbles constantly moved by the waves offer no foothold for plants, nor hiding place for animals. Yet a few still manage to survive on every shingle beach.

because of such conditions that so few animals live on shingle beaches and from an animal point of view, they are close to being ecological deserts.

If, however, the beach is composed of larger, orange-sized stones there will be crevices between them where small animals can find both shelter and living space. Such beaches usually have a good deal of silt and mud which tends to fill these crevices, and then you may find species that normally favour mud, living there.

The lugworm, *Arenicola ecaudata*, is a worm that sometimes settles in such situations.

Sandhoppers are found on shingle beaches. One which lives under stones on both rocky and sandy shores and is also common in shingle is *Gammarus locusta*. Farther up the beach, where the seaweed smothers the strandline, another sandhopper (*Talitrus saltator*) feeds on the rotting vegetation. If you pull some of the seaweed aside, you will see them in quantity. Here too you may find a

*Above*: Sea campion grows on shingle banks and cliffs, and flowers between June and August. It has thick, waxy leaves, with a mat of non-flowering shoots.

*Below*: As more and more people enjoy the seashore, space for nesting birds grows less, so reserves are essential.

TERNS NESTING

PLEASE AVOID AREA BETWEEN POSTS

grey and hairy fly about 4 millimetres in length. It is the kelp fly (*Coelopa frigida*) and its larvae will be found living in the moist, rotting seaweed.

Towards the top of the beach there will almost certainly be plants such as sea campion (*Silene maritima*), yellow horned-poppy (*Glaucium flavum*), sea couch (*Agropyron pungens*) and shrubby sea-blite (*Suaeda* spp).

Where shingle has become stabilized, and providing it is well away from human disturbance, seabirds often use it as a nesting site. In consequence, a few selected sites have been made into nature reserves, simply because of the amount of birds that nest there.

Sandwich terns (*Sterna sandvicensis*) and other tern species together with ringed plovers (*Charadrius hiaticula*) and oystercatchers (*Haematopus ostralegus*) may be seen during the nesting season. Quite naturally, that is the time of year when the wardens of nature reserves are less keen to have too many visitors. Many species of seabirds are having difficulty in finding suitable nesting places because of the way man is taking over the shore, so the few remaining ones are well guarded by naturalists. Many such reserves use volunteer wardens during the nesting season, simply to help ensure that the birds succeed in raising a family.

Birds are also cared for by the RSPB (The Royal Society for the Protection of Birds). Here a bird with an injured wing is being tended.

Here is a selection of plants and animals that live on shingle beaches.

# Shingle beach

**SANDHOPPERS**

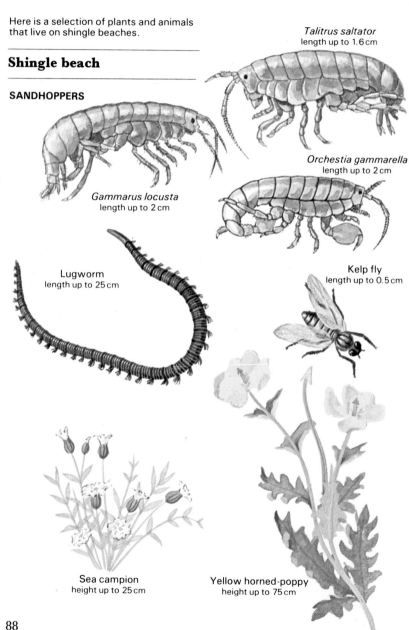

*Talitrus saltator*
length up to 1.6 cm

*Gammarus locusta*
length up to 2 cm

*Orchestia gammarella*
length up to 2 cm

Lugworm
length up to 25 cm

Kelp fly
length up to 0.5 cm

Sea campion
height up to 25 cm

Yellow horned-poppy
height up to 75 cm

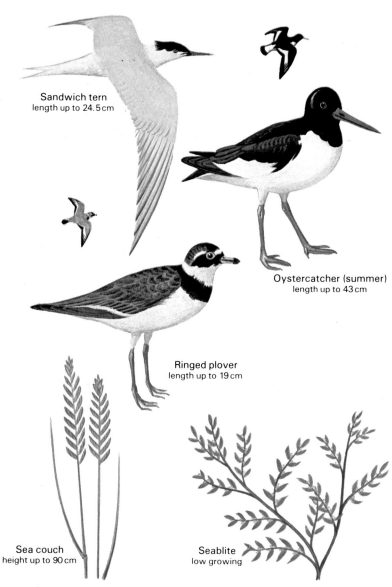

Sandwich tern
length up to 24.5 cm

Oystercatcher (summer)
length up to 43 cm

Ringed plover
length up to 19 cm

Sea couch
height up to 90 cm

Seablite
low growing

# Estuaries

When exploring muddy estuaries, be careful. Always go with an experienced adult who knows when and where to walk. Such areas vary tremendously from long stretches of muddy sand through gravelly mussel beds to pure mud.

Estuaries offer great opportunities for exploration. They are great spots for bird-watching throughout the year, a host of wonderfully adapted animals live in and on the mud mostly hidden from sight by camouflage or by living below the surface, and many interesting plants will be found along the banks and in the marshes that usually border estuaries.

## Mudflats

According to location, you will find sea-lettuce and one or two small wracks attached to occasional stones, or even finding holdfast security where the mud is more solid.

### Hydrobia

One animal that has found its ideal home on mud is a small spire shell called *Hydrobia ulvae* and is usually less than 5 millimetres long. To find them, you will have to look for areas of mud covered with a green seaweed known as *Enteromorpha*. This is one of their food plants and where this tiny snail is abundant, you may find as many as 100 000 to a square metre. Indeed, they are so common that they look like gravel spread thickly over the mud surface.

It is interesting that this tiny snail, which by itself can hardly be seen, exists in such astronomical numbers as to form an important part of the diet of many seabirds.

You may have noticed how small waders follow the edge of the rising and ebbing tides. This is partly due to the habits of *Hydrobia*. As the tide begins to rise, the animal comes out of the little burrow it made at low tide, and produces a minute 'raft' from mucus. This 'raft' floats on the underside of the surface of the water, spreading a little way all around the foot of *Hydrobia*. So, as the tide rises, it moves up the shore and then, as it ebbs, back it goes once more – or at least, the survivors do.

*Hydrobia* is a good example of how one species is inter-meshed with many others. You can probably imagine the effects of an oil slick on their populations, and how this would affect the feeding of waders. Similarly if other forms of pollution are present in the estuary, each *Hydrobia* may absorb a tiny fragment, but for a wader eating hundreds of *Hydrobia*, the amount of the toxic stuff taken in may be enough to kill it. It's an example of how one species can die by feeding on poisons eaten by another.

### Peppery furrow shell

Mud is the home of a large bivalve, the peppery furrow shell (*Scrobicularia plana*), and to find this mollusc, you must look for a small hole at the centre of star-shaped grooves. It looks rather as if a small, spoked wheel has been pushed against the mud. The grooves are caused by the long syphon of the furrow shell, as it searches for food and takes in water.

The furrow shell lives a few centimetres down in a permanent burrow. It does not need to move, because there is so much food constantly arriving all around it.

With a fork or spade, you can dig a few up. Wash them clean and put them in a plastic beaker or similar container. At first, their syphons will be withdrawn inside the shells, but wait a little while, and things will begin to happen. First you will see the tips of the syphons show a little way out of the shells. A short time after this, they grow longer, and then finally, if the animal is not disturbed, the semi-translucent syphon tubes will almost fill the container. If the container is placed so that the light is coming from behind it, and if you carefully look at the open ends of these syphons, you will see food particles being sucked into them.

Peppery furrow shells in a jar of estuary water quickly extend their syphons.

## Corophium

Another attractive yet strange little animal is the amphipod (*Corophium volutator*). You will find it in soft mud banks, providing there is some freshwater mingling with the seawater.

Some 5 to 8 millimetres long, it lives in burrows that can be as deep as 10 centimetres.

As you can probably imagine, maintaining a burrow and keeping it open in soft mud is no easy matter, but *Corophium* does it by giving off a special substance which strengthens the walls of the burrow. When the tide is in, it comes out of its burrow, and walks around looking for pieces of plants and animals which it then eats.

## Ragworms

If you dig up a forkful of mud, and slowly break it apart, you will most likely find a ragworm (*Nereis* spp). Indeed, in suitable places, they live in large numbers, and 20 in a forkful is not uncommon. They live in burrows, and come out when the tide is in, and crawl around, feeding on any creature small enough to seize and swallow. They make excellent fishing baits and you may see anglers digging for them.

## Peacock worm

In very sheltered places will be found the beautiful peacock worm (*Sabella pavonina*). It's a tube worm, which builds a tube about 35 centimetres long, from grains of fine sand and mud. Leave it undisturbed in an aquarium, and you will see it open out. It does this very slowly, and reminds me of a rocket bursting into stars as its circle of brightly coloured tentacles unfold. Beautiful as they are, their main function is to collect

The peacock worm lives in a firm, muddy tube up to 30 centimetres long. The ring of tentacles collects food from the water.

drifting food particles, for each tentacle is fringed with tiny hairs that form a dense network.

## Eel grass beds

Fine mud grades off into muddy sand, and wherever the balance is just right, and providing the site is sheltered, eel grass (*Zostera* spp) will grow. It is of particular interest, because it is a marine *flowering* plant, and not a seaweed, although it lives in the sea. Where it grows in quantity, it covers the seabed like long grass, and this gives it another popular name of sea-grass. As a habitat, it provides ideal living space for a rich variety of creatures.

## Pipefish

Pipefish (Syngnathidae) seem to find it much to their liking and a snorkelling swim through such an area can be very rewarding. You will notice that pipefish have long tube-like mouths which open at the extreme end, and their method of feeding is quite interesting. They hunt small prawns, shrimps and other tiny active creatures, following every movement of their prey, until they are within 2 centimetres of it. Then, a sudden intake of water sucks the prey in, and the pipefish snap their jaws shut on it. So loud is this action that in an aquarium, you can actually hear it.

Sometimes when feeding, pipefish turn on their side, or even upside-down before seizing prey. Like many other fish, they single out their prey and follow it until they are in just the right position to seize it.

In the summer months, pipefish produce their young. The female lays her eggs, which are then carried by the male until their time for hatching. Some species do this by attaching the eggs by a kind of glue to their undersides. The male of another species even has a special pouch on its belly into which the eggs fit. When the young first hatch, they are like tiny mobile pins, and if frightened, will return to the male's pouch for protection.

Incidentally, pipefish can be kept in aquaria, providing you can offer them plenty of small, live food.

*Above*: The male worm pipefish cares for the eggs. He carries them, glued in rows, on his belly.

*Below*: The common cuttlefish is a fascinating animal. It is an expert at colour change and can learn.

## Cuttlefish

In summer, *Zostera* beds can be searched for the eggs of the cuttlefish (*Sepia officinalis*). They look rather like bunches of small black grapes, and are fairly common, because cuttlefish thrive in such places. The cuttlefish is a sea-creature which is related to the octopus. It has eight sucker-bearing arms and two longer ones which it can shoot out to capture shrimps and small fish. It also eats crabs, and to catch these, it attacks from behind, and smothers them with its tentacles. When hunting shrimps, it blows out small jets of water from a tube below its head. This disturbs the shrimps which are buried in the sand, and as soon as they move, the cuttlefish seizes them.

## Muddy sand

The muddy sand itself is the home of a variety of burrowing molluscs.

### Gaper

Largest of these is the gaper (*Mya arenaria*) which is a truly magnificent shell as large as 15 by 7 centimetres. Living deep down, they have extremely long syphons which, due to their large bulk, even when drawn back, cause the shell to gape. Hence, the popular name, gaper.

### Otter shell

Another massive mollusc to be found in sandy mud is the otter shell (*Lutraria lutraria*) which inhabits the area on and below low spring tide level. Apart from the syphon holes, another indication of its presence is one or two empty shells on the tide line, or odd ones, sometimes spread along the beach. The shell valves are quite delicate, and after gales, you will occasionally find hundreds of the shells lying broken on the tide line. That's when the gulls move in to feast.

### Netted dogwhelk

There are few univalves to be found here, but one species, the netted dogwhelk (*Nassarius reticulatus*), finds the situation ideal for its way of life. Being a whelk, it has a long syphon which sticks upwards, well above the shell and the creature also has a very broad and flat foot on which it crawls through the muddy sand. With its syphon well up in the clear water above the sand level, it can draw in clean water for breathing, whilst its body is immersed in quite smelly and dirty surroundings.

Netted dogwhelks are useful aquarium inhabitants, because they are scavengers and will clear up any pieces of food left lying on the bottom. Also, their movement through the sand helps to keep it 'ploughed up' and aerated, thus avoiding troublesome bacterial action caused by dirt.

**Baiting for netted dogwhelks** Netted dogwhelks have a keen sense of smell, so an easy way to catch these molluscs is to set baits at low tide. Ask your fishmonger for some flatfish skeletons, but before you set off, make about 18 wire pegs. Use *thick* galvanized wire, and cut it into lengths of about 25 centimetres. Bend the top few centimetres over to form a hook.

Good places to bait are the edge of a harbour wall or muddy sand near rocks. Simply place the fish skeleton flat on the sand and anchor it there by pressing the wire pegs through it until the hook presses down on the bone. Put the baits about 9 metres apart, and leave them out until low tide next day. In the morning you will find dogwhelks gathered around or buried in the sand near the fish skeleton. Collect some of them and remember to take the wire pegs home too.

**Carpet shell**
Mud grades into muddy sand, and that in turn, into muddy gravel. This is the home of a common bivalve, the carpet shell (*Venerupis pullastra*). It burrows quite deeply, and is a suspension feeder, feeding on tiny particles of drifting food which it sucks in with its long syphon.

**Common cockle**
In the sandier parts of many estuaries are cockle beds, areas where the common cockle (*Cerastoderma*

Netted dogwhelks with a dead crab. They are perfect scavengers, with long flexible syphons to detect food.

*edule*) lives in vast numbers, often exceeding 1000 per square metre. They feed through their syphons, drawing in plant debris, microscopic plants, and a few very small animals such as larval crabs.

Unlike some other molluscs, cockles are either male or female, although the difference can only be discovered by dissecting the foot for identification of the sperm and eggs.

**Estimating age** Cockles grow throughout the year, up to about 5 centimetres, but growth is usually greatly reduced in winter. At this time, the edge of the shell grows thicker, thus forming a ring each winter. By counting these rings, you can estimate the age of the cockle.

**Enemies** The main predators on cockles are marine fish such as flounders and plaice, shore crabs, and starfish which eat the small ones. Gulls and oystercatchers eat the larger ones, although normally, gulls pick up only those that have been brought to the surface by a storm or similar disturbance.

Oystercatchers seem to prefer cockles of about two years old. They take them out of the sand, carry them to a selected patch of harder sand, and hammer them open with their beak. You will spot some of these 'feeding piles' of empty, broken shells, where oystercatchers are numerous. Incidentally, one oystercatcher can eat 500 cockles in a day! Next time you pick up a cockle, try to see it in terms of total population, and the vast numbers consumed

each year. It is indeed a very important shellfish.

## Oysters

Many estuaries make ideal places for oysters. In Europe, there are two important species, the British native oyster (*Ostrea edulis*) and the Portuguese oyster (*Crassostrea angulata*).

Native oysters (*Ostrea edulis*) alternate in sex, starting life as males and then changing to females. At spawning time, the males release sperms into the sea, and as soon as one does this, triggered by a water temperature of 10°C, the entire oyster bed follows suit. Fertilization of the eggs occurs when female oysters containing eggs draw in sperms through their syphons. The eggs are held in the females' bodies and develop into 0·2 millimetre long larvae which are set free into the sea.

In contrast, the Portuguese oyster (*Crassostrea angulata*) females liberate their *eggs* into the sea. A single female may release as many as 100 000 000 (one hundred million) eggs.

Eventually, after a short larval life drifting in the plankton, the larvae settle and the fortunate ones cement themselves to stones, shells and rocks. The others, lacking footholds, die.

Man has learned how to cultivate oysters, and the story, although fascinating, does not come within the scope of this book. However, you might like to get a book from your library, and read all about it.

## Birds

Estuaries and mudflats are wonderful places for birdwatching, although it is often difficult to get close enough, so binoculars will be useful. Each species that comes here to feed has its own range of food species, and their methods of feeding vary.

### Shelduck (*Tadorna tadorna*)
These birds feed on the tiny snail, *Hydrobia*, which they gather by walking slowly forward and swinging their beaks to left and right through the surface of the mud. The zig-zag marks left in the mud are a sign of their work.

### Godwits (*Limosa* spp) and curlews (*Numenius* spp)
These birds have very long curved beaks, which they use to probe deep into the mud to catch worms and some small molluscs.

### Oystercatcher (*Haematopus ostralegus*)
With their bright red beaks and black and white colouring, these are familiar birds of estuaries, and their calls are very much part of these great open spaces. Where mussel beds abound, oystercatchers feed

*Below left:* The shelduck sweeps its beak from side to side through the mud to pick up algae and small animals.

*Below right*: The curlew uses its beak to probe deeper for worms and small shellfish.

well, although they also eat other molluscs, crabs, worms and insects. Perhaps a little unexpectedly for a wader, they will occasionally swim across pools if the water is too deep for wading.

## Redshanks and greenshanks
(*Tringa* spp)
These are among the smaller waders. They have medium length bills and are able to reach down for worms and molluscs, a little below the surface. They also eat insects and even small fish.

## Turnstone (*Arenaria interpres*)
Groups of these birds usually fly in to feed as the tide ebbs. Their common name suggests their method of feeding, but they also move fronds of seaweed in their search for small molluscs and sandhoppers.

## Brent goose (*Branta bernicla*)
These come into such areas to browse on the eel grass, but they are shy birds and keep well away from populated areas.

## Other birds you may see
In estuaries other birds you may see include plovers (*Pluvialis* and *Charadrius* spp), sanderlings (*Calidris alba*), dunlins (*Calidris alpina*), and sandpipers (*Calidris* spp).

So, you can see how each species has its own method of feeding, and because of this, they can all find plentiful food in the estuary. There is very little competition, but occa-sionally, in hard winters, their food becomes 'locked up' due to freezing mud. Their beaks can no longer penetrate to gather the worms and molluscs, and many birds die from hunger.

There's an interesting little twist to this, for land birds that live along the shores of the estuary have the same problem. The thrush (*Turdus* spp) normally breaks and eats snails, but in a freeze-up there are no snails as they are all hidden or frozen in. So, estuary bank thrushes go down to the water's edge, and break up winkles. They are able to do this, because the shells of estuary winkles are much thinner than sea-shore ones, due to a lack of lime. This is an example of a bird making use of an alternative food, which could not be easily eaten by waders with unsuitable bills.

With so many birds present, it is not surprising that these muddy places are criss-crossed with tracks of all kinds. So one of your activities here can be making plaster casts of some of them. (See page 132.) As you wander around, you will see cormorants (*Phalacrocorax carbo*) flying off up river to look for freshwater fish, or you may spot one or two standing on the edge of the tide, holding their wings open to dry.

Once the tide turns and starts to rise, all the birds are slowly driven towards the shore, and then, one by one, and sometimes in flocks, the waders fly up and away to quiet, sheltered banks or islands to rest.

*Above*: The oystercatcher's beak is a perfect tool for opening shellfish.

*Below*: The turnstone finds animals like the sandhopper (*inset*) under stone and seaweed.

Here is a selection of animals that live
in estuaries.

## Mudflats

*Hydrobia ulvae*
shell up to 0.6 cm high

Baltic tellin
shell up to 2.5 cm long

Cross-cut carpet shell
shell up to 5 cm long

*Gastrana fragilis*
shell up to 4.5 cm long

*Corophium volutator*
length up to 0.8 cm

Rag worm
length up to 12 cm

King rag worm
length up to 20 cm

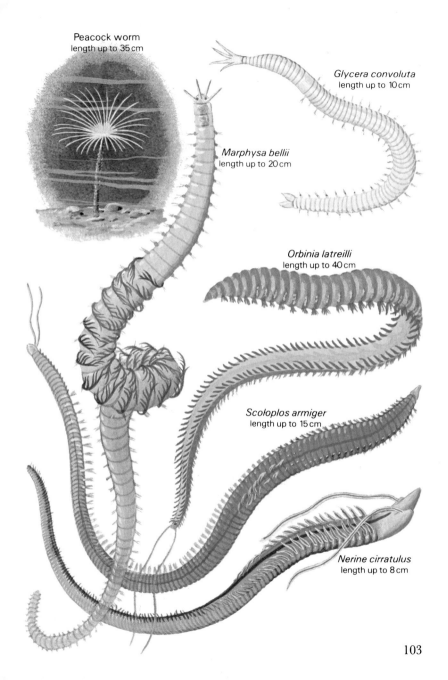

Peacock worm
length up to 35 cm

*Glycera convoluta*
length up to 10 cm

*Marphysa bellii*
length up to 20 cm

*Orbinia latreilli*
length up to 40 cm

*Scoloplos armiger*
length up to 15 cm

*Nerine cirratulus*
length up to 8 cm

103

# Eel grass beds

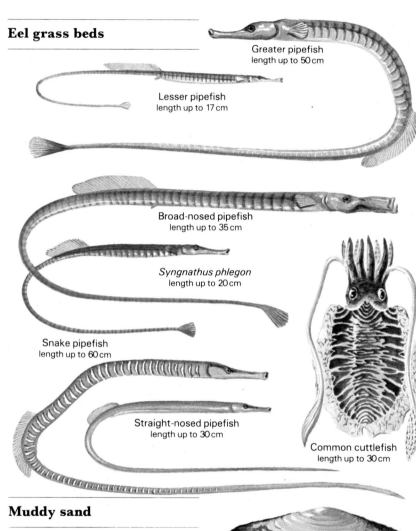

Greater pipefish
length up to 50 cm

Lesser pipefish
length up to 17 cm

Broad-nosed pipefish
length up to 35 cm

*Syngnathus phlegon*
length up to 20 cm

Snake pipefish
length up to 60 cm

Straight-nosed pipefish
length up to 30 cm

Common cuttlefish
length up to 30 cm

# Muddy sand

Sand gaper
shell up to 15 cm long

Common otter shell
shell up to 12.5 cm long

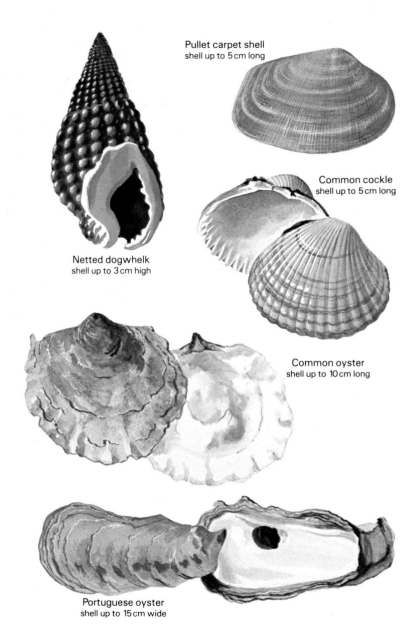

Pullet carpet shell
shell up to 5 cm long

Netted dogwhelk
shell up to 3 cm high

Common cockle
shell up to 5 cm long

Common oyster
shell up to 10 cm long

Portuguese oyster
shell up to 15 cm wide

105

# Birds

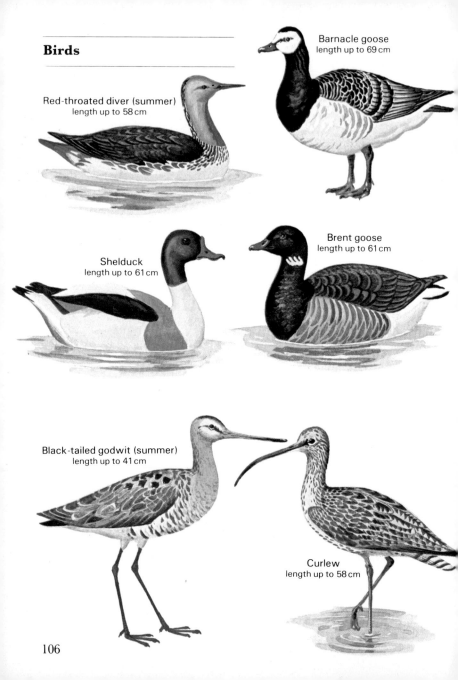

Barnacle goose
length up to 69 cm

Red-throated diver (summer)
length up to 58 cm

Shelduck
length up to 61 cm

Brent goose
length up to 61 cm

Black-tailed godwit (summer)
length up to 41 cm

Curlew
length up to 58 cm

Whimbrel
length up to 41 cm

Greenshank
length up to 30.5 cm

Turnstone (summer)
length up to 23 cm

Sanderling (summer)
length up to 20 cm

Dunlin (summer)
length up to 19 cm

Knot (winter)
length up to 25 cm

Wigeon (male)
length up to 51 cm

# Strandlines

When you first walk on to a beach it may seem to be a flat stretch of sand with nothing more than multi-coloured deckchairs and sunbathers, and in winter it may look much less inviting. But look again and you will almost certainly see a darker line weaving its way into the distance. Sometimes there may be more than one, the highest being near the very

The strandline changes daily as fresh flotsam and jetsam is left by the tides. Here are found jellyfish drifted ashore, crabshells, shells and many kinds of egg cases. Winter is often the best time to search the strandline, especially after a storm. But whatever the season or time of day, a walk along the edge of the sea will always reveal something of interest.

top of the beach where only the highest tides or biggest storm waves reach.

These are strandlines, the place where the sea strands all manner of items from plastic sheets to egg cases; from driftwood to broken crab pots; from bottles to bird skeletons. Some-times referred to as flotsam and jet-sam these objects are the remains of living and non-living things washed up by the sea. Once in a while, a particularly violent storm may tear away at cliffs and dislodge great trees or even sink ships which finish up on the beach you are searching.

# Searching for eggs

When you have come down on to a beach and seen the strandline, the first thing to do is walk slowly along it and look carefully, for many of the best items will be covered by seaweed. Push this seaweed aside with your foot or use a piece of driftwood to probe deeper.

## Common whelk

Start your search at the top of the beach where you will probably find light objects such as the egg capsules of the common whelk (*Buccinum undatum*). After the tide goes out, these egg masses quickly dry out and a sea wind often rolls them up the beach. They vary in size from that of a small apple to nearly as large as a soccer ball, and are made up of small capsules. They were laid in deeper water by the common whelk, and some of the larger masses are the result of several whelks laying their eggs together.

Each capsule once contained as many as 12 eggs and each of these slowly grew into a tiny whelk. The first ones out of the egg immediately set upon the unhatched ones and ate them so that perhaps only two or three finally crawled out of each capsule. If you count the number of capsules in an egg mass, you will gain some idea of the total number of whelks that were born from it.

If you are very fortunate, you may find a freshly stranded mass of egg capsules with some eggs still inside them. At other times, if you gently shake the capsules on to a piece of paper, you may find a few tiny whelk shells for your collection. Most capsule masses will be crisp and dry, but if not, you can quickly dry them out in the open air. It is a good idea to rinse them under a tap to remove any salt which tends to attract moisture and causes dampness which may eventually rot your specimens.

## The mermaid's purse

Another egg capsule which is often washed up on the beach, is the mermaid's purse. There are two main kinds. The first kind is rather squarish with a thick horn-like projection from each corner of the capsule. This is the egg capsule of one of the many different kinds of skates or rays which live in the offshore water. The second kind is more oblong in shape with twining tendrils from the corners and is the egg capsule of one of the dogfish.

The female dogfish lays a small number of eggs in winter. The eggs develop within her body, where they are fertilized by the male. Slowly, the eggs develop and a capsule grows around each one. The female dogfish then slowly forces a capsule from her body, and for a little while it trails behind her, joined to her body by long elastic threads. Next, she swims down to the seabed and searches for a suitable growing seaweed plant. Having found one, she

The female common whelk turns slowly around as she lays her egg capsules and so they form these large masses. Any firm object such as a tyre may be used as a base for the capsules.

swims around and around the plant until the trailing threads and the capsule become wrapped firmly around it. The egg now fixed to the seaweed begins a seven to nine months growth.

A capsule is about 5 centimetres across. Inside is a yellow yolk on which is a tiny life spot. This spot grows until after about a month it has developed into a perfect tiny dogfish, and from its belly a network of blood vessels spread all over the yolk carrying this food back into the body of the baby fish. By about the seventh month, the yolk has nearly all been absorbed, and the dogfish almost fills the egg case. When it is completely developed it gives a strong wriggle and bursts out of the capsule to swim away.

If you look carefully at a mermaid's purse which has been washed up, you should be able to see the opening through which the little fish escaped into the sea.

111

## Necklace shells

Another interesting egg mass to be found on certain sandy beaches is the egg 'collar' of a necklace shell, *Natica*. This shellfish lays its eggs and reinforces them with sand grains, whilst the newly exposed surface also becomes sand covered. You will often find these washed ashore after a storm.

---

## Stranded timber and shells

### Shipworm

Stranded timber of all kinds is common on the strandline and some of the larger thicker pieces should be examined for holes made by the shipworm (*Teredo* spp). There are several species of this creature which is in fact a mollusc. Starting life in the plankton, the young shipworms settle on to drifting wood, pier piles or any timber in the sea, and attach themselves to it by a thin thread. After a little while they grip, or rather suck, on to the wood surface and slowly turn themselves back and forth through half a circle. As they do so, the saw edge of their shells begins to wear away the wood. Boring at a rate of 2 centimetres a day, a shipworm eats the sawdust and grows. At the same time it sucks in water containing drifting food particles which give it a little variety in its diet. There are few animals in the world that are able to digest wood but *Teredo* does it most successfully.

Since there are many in any piece of infected wood, it is perhaps surprising that no two burrowers ever run into one another. By means unknown to us, the *Teredo* knows when it is nearing another burrow and either changes direction or stops tunnelling. If it stops for any length of time it puts down a thin coating of lime around its burrow, and continues to live and reproduce in this.

During the days of the wooden ships, *Teredo* flourished and many a man-of-war that survived the guns of enemy ships was finally sunk by this mollusc, as its timbers collapsed due to the vast number of tunnels within them.

If you find a piece of timber with holes in it, take it home and split the

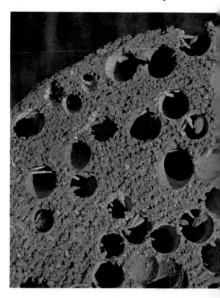

wood down the grain. You will then be able to see the borings and, even better, collect a few shells of the extraordinary little animal.

## Gribble
Very small holes in timber are made by the gribble (*Limnoria lignorum*), a woodlouse-like creature about 4 millimetres long which is a type of crustacean. It bites its way into timber but only goes in a little way, usually about 5 millimetres before boring parallel to the surface of the wood for about 25 millimetres. A single female gribble may produce as many as 30 young, and these

The shell valves of *Teredo* are shaped to cut into wood. This large log which floated on to the beach has been sawn in half to show the burrows.

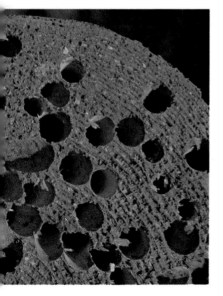

immediately begin to make small burrows beside those of their parents.

With a pest like this eating away at pier piles and wharf supports, it is only natural that man has tried a number of methods of controlling them. One method is to detonate some explosive near to the infected wood and this kills the gribble by vibration!

## Boring sponge
If there are oyster shells washed up, take a closer look at some of them. Almost certainly, you will discover many of them are riddled with small holes and thin burrows. These were made by the boring sponge (*Cliona celata*) which lived on the shell when it was on the seabed. It's a soft, yellow sponge when alive, and it gives off an acid which eats away the limestone of the shell, and into these holes, the sponge expands and grows. If a rough sea washes the shell ashore, the sponge dies in the air, its body breaks up and all that is left are the tiny holes where once it lived.

## Goose barnacle
Stranded timber is occasionally inhabited by a cluster of goose barnacles (*Lepas anatifera*), which unfortunately are usually dead, having been killed by exposure to the air. When alive, they hang down from the floating wood, their white plates open, and out sweeps a hand-shaped network of filaments. These catch small drifting particles in the

sea and lift them back into the mouth of the barnacle.

Goose barnacles also fix themselves to floating bottles where they usually group around the stopper. I have also found them on the brass plug end of an electric bulb and on the old glass-ball floats once used by trawlermen.

## Cuttlebones and squid shells

Among the debris on the strandline will be pieces of cuttlebone. These are not really bone, but in fact the soft internal shells of cuttlefish. Most of the pieces on the beach will have peck marks made by birds' beaks, for many birds enjoy the rich, limey deposits, and for that reason, pieces of cuttlebone are sold in pet shops for feeding to budgerigars, canaries and other caged birds.

On rare occasions, you may find the shell of a squid. It is a most delicate thing, and looks rather like a transparent plastic feather. It is all that is left of a dead squid, a creature similar in many ways to a cuttlefish. Both of them have evolved into swimming creatures which, in short bursts of speed, are probably the fastest sea animals. Both cuttlebone and squid shells will make interesting additions to your seashore museum.

A bottle thrown into the sea has become the home of goose barnacles which settled on to it out of the plankton.

By searching you may find remains of an edible crab that has moulted.

With a little care by Man, fewer seabirds would die by pollution.

## Crab shells

Dead crabs are not uncommon along the strandline, and according to the locality of the beach, so the species will differ. On sandy shores, you may find masked crabs (*Corystes cassivelaunus*), whilst on rocky shores, the common shore crab (*Carcinus maenas*) will be more common.

All crabs are a bit of a problem if you want to keep them as dead specimens, for they quickly begin to smell most unpleasant. The best time to collect them is in the summer, for then they dry out on the hot sand very soon after being stranded.

If you want to do a little detective work, you can search carefully for pieces of crab. They are common on the shore, and once you learn to recognize them, you will find legs, bodies and certainly plenty of their cast backs. Try to sort them out,

and discover where the pieces fitted on the crab, and how many different kinds you can collect. Collecting perfect backs is by no means easy, for they are delicate, and break very quickly when cast ashore. But then, half the fun in beachcombing is looking for better and better specimens to replace some of those tatty ones you started with.

## Birds

Dead seabirds are not uncommon on the shore, and it's a good plan to examine their legs to see if they have been ringed. With the increase in the scientific study of birds, more and more are being marked with rings on their legs. Each ring is a valuable record of that particular bird's life story. If you do find such rings, you can send them to a natural history museum. Include with the ring a note of your name and address, date and place of find, species (if known) and any other details you consider of value. By doing that, you will be helping research, and often you will receive details back from the ringing organization.

The strandline is a fine place to start collecting feathers. Most of these have come from moulting sea-birds, and if you watch a flock of gulls at rest on the shore, you will see they spend a great deal of time preening. This activity also removes feathers, which you can collect. Collect only the very best, and if you find it a problem to sort out which species of bird they came from, a visit to your local museum may be of help. If they have a collection of birds, you will be able to take your feathers along, and match them up with the specimens on display.

Tests of the edible sea urchin (top) and the green sea urchin.

## Sea urchin tests

Most delicate of all stranded trea-sures are the tests or external shells of sea urchins. When you find some of these, be particularly careful with them, for they are most delicate. You will probably be wise to carry them home in a small box with crumpled paper to keep them safe. Dried and given a coat of clear matt polyurethane to strengthen them, they will make a unique addition to your collection.

It is possible to buy the melon-sized tests of the edible urchin in gift shops, and there is a consider-able trade in these beautiful objects. But the urchins were collected alive by divers and killed purely for the value of their tests as souvenirs. From a conservation point of view, it is a trade that should be dis-couraged.

## Making your own seashore museum

A collection of flotsam and jetsam

makes a good start for a small seashore museum, and all the individual pieces can be displayed by using simple and cheap materials.

Egg cases need to be dried thoroughly by leaving them in an airy situation until they are quite crisp. If you like a shiny finish, you can varnish them with a clear glossy polyurethane varnish, or else use a matt polyurethane to give a non-shiny surface.

Timber should be allowed to dry in the open air. You can then split it or saw it into cross sections. Leave it with its natural surface, as this always looks better than a varnished finish.

Cuttlebones and crabs' legs and backs need little care, except drying. But beware of any dead, complete crabs, for they are not easy to preserve without the use of rather dangerous chemicals, and are best left on the shore.

Feathers need a little gentle attention with a soft paintbrush to clean them up. Bones of all kinds look much better after bleaching. Use ordinary household bleach and mix a strong solution in the bottom of a bucket. Be very careful as bleach can seriously burn you. Ask an adult to help you. Place the bones in this and leave them for a day before washing out the bleach in several changes of tapwater. Leave the bones in a dry place until all moisture has gone, and you will be quite surprised at the clean, white appearance of your specimens.

**Preparing a skate egg case for display**

1. Leave egg case to dry thoroughly.

2. Paint with clear polyurethane varnish.

SKATE EGG CASE
Combe Cove, Dipsey
August 20th 1981

3. Exhibit with simple labelling.

## Mounting and display

If you have some space to lay out your specimens, you will need to think about the general display. Most objects look best on pieces of clean card to which they can be fixed with a good glue, or wired into place with thin wire. Whilst a number of different egg capsules can be mounted as a single display on one piece of card, *Teredo* might look better on its own.

The best way to get ideas for display is to take a look around a good museum, for there you will see all kinds of mounting and novel ways of displaying specimens to best advantage. Simple stands for single objects can be made by upending yoghurt or cream cartons and all kinds of kitchen packings will come in useful. Card can be cut from cornflake, detergent or food packets and the reverse, unprinted side is often a good colour for display. Odd pieces of hardboard are even better, but of course, cost money. Scraps of wood and plastic sheeting should be saved too, because you will need a large variety of mounting boards as your collection grows.

## Labelling and captions

All specimens should be plainly labelled with their name, the place where the specimen was found, and the date. A few sentences of interesting facts can then be added together with some drawings, photographs or coloured pictures related to the exhibit. Always remember that it is the *object* that is important, and this must be given pride of place. Too much writing tends to take attention away from it.

As your collection grows, you will probably find the need to refer to more and more books. No doubt you will buy the occasional reference book, and so build up your own library.

## New displays all the time

Finally, try to change your collection by redisplaying it and by putting in new exhibits as often as you can. You will find it necessary to clean up and repair some exhibits and the museum experts refer to this work as conservation.

Remember too, there is always new flotsam and jetsam being stranded on the shore, and always the chance of some new and exciting specimen to be found such as pieces of sponge, starfish, fish and animal bones, stranded jellyfish, indeed the list is endless.

It is the ever present possibility of discovering a stranded porpoise, part of a shipwreck, or some strange and exotic creature like a turtle, that makes beachcombing so exciting. Of one thing you can be certain, there is always something new to discover on every beach you visit.

typical label

# MUSSEL
## (MYTILUS EDULIS)

Combe Cove Dipchurch
August 20th. 1981.

**Different ways of mounting specimens**

upturned yoghurt pot

label

TEREDO
(TEREDO NAVALIS
BALL~ DIVALI
~JUNE 20. 1971)

Clean printing from the yoghurt pot with steel wool.

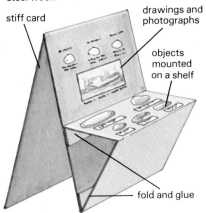

stiff card

drawings and photographs

objects mounted on a shelf

fold and glue

Use two pieces of card of the same width — one piece ⅔rds the length of the other.

*Left*: A stranded lesser rorqual whale.

Here is a selection of objects that you may find on the strandline.

## Common finds on the strandline

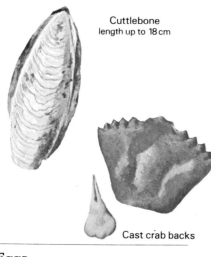

Cuttlebone
length up to 18 cm

Cast crab backs

Compass jellyfish
diameter up to 30 cm

## Eggs

Lesser spotted dogfish and egg capsule
egg capsule up to 6 cm long

Common whelk and egg mass
egg mass up to 13 cm in diameter

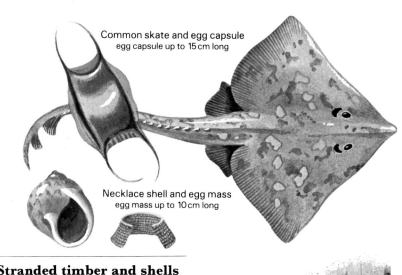

Common skate and egg capsule
egg capsule up to 15 cm long

Necklace shell and egg mass
egg mass up to 10 cm long

## Stranded timber and shells

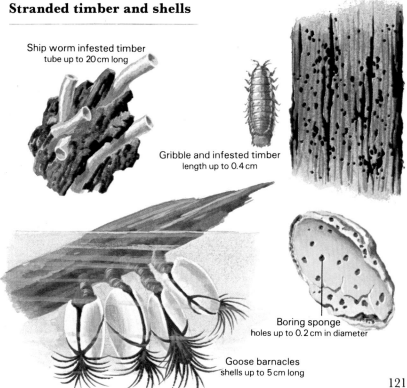

Ship worm infested timber
tube up to 20 cm long

Gribble and infested timber
length up to 0.4 cm

Boring sponge
holes up to 0.2 cm in diameter

Goose barnacles
shells up to 5 cm long

# The edge of the sea

The coastline of Europe is infinitely varied. In some places there are cliffs, in others, sand dunes. Rocky platforms alternate with sandy beaches, while in other areas there are shingle beaches, stony beaches or rocky beaches.

But whatever the nature of the coast you are near, there is always a narrow band of coast that shares both the sea and the land. The nearer you go towards the sea the more marine are the species you will meet. The farther inland you go the more species will be land types.

Generally speaking, coasts are exposed and windy places, and much of the vegetation that grows there is wind-pruned and often quite sparse. Gorse (*Ulex europaeus*) that grows to over 2 metres tall inland, may be less than 25 centimetres on the coast; bluebells (*Endymion nonscriptus*) growing on sloping cliff sites have flower stalks less than 10 centimetres tall, whereas they grow more than 45 centimetres tall inland.

On the cliffs and dunes live a great
many different kinds of wild flowers.
Most of them will only be found in
this narrow margin between the
seashore and the land.

# The land margins

Most creatures to be found on the shore have descended from previous generations that lived entirely in the sea. For one reason or another, through the ages, a few have come out of the sea to live above the tidal zone. Animals such as the small periwinkle are thought to be slowly invading the land, for even now they inhabit rocks above and in the splash zone, and only resort to the sea for spawning.

## Rabbit

The rabbit (*Oryctolagus cuniculus*) is a common animal and has established itself all along the coasts. Many live in shallow burrows in bramble and gorse thickets, whilst others seem to prefer the deeper burrows dug into the actual cliffside.

## Rats

Rats (Muridae) are not uncommon on the top of the beach and although seldom seen, they scavenge picnic scraps after dark. They are highly suspicious animals, and extremely wary. The tracks with the familiar 'drag' mark of the tail will be found on the sand as a sign that they are about. When gales strand dead creatures, the rats quickly take advantage of the situation. In general they seem to inhabit the less developed beaches, places without promenades, and are usually found where rocks offer shelter.

## Mink

Another species that is beginning to spread along parts of the coast is the mink (*Mustela vison*). Originally the wild population began with escaped animals from fur farms, and in some places they have become a pest in rivers. When short of food they come down to estuaries and the coast, anywhere in fact where they can find a meal. Fish is their main diet.

## Fox

Another predator which visits the margin of the sea is the fox (*Vulpes vulpes*). They come for rabbits and in places where seabirds nest on dunes and in fields bordering estuaries they sometimes wreak havoc when they go on a killing mission.

Some foxes even enlarge rabbit burrows and settle down in coastal earths, probably to be near to a good supply of food and relatively safe from human disturbance.

## Voles and shrews

Smaller mammals abound in the grass and if you search in the tangled undergrowth you will find the tunnels used by voles and shrews. They are easily recognized by being less than 2·5 centimetres in diameter, and are formed simply by the small mammals constantly running through the grass.

According to the habitat so you will find the bank vole (*Clethrionomys glareolus*) and the field vole (*Microtus agrestis*). All voles are herbivores

Rabbits burrow into sand dunes and move a considerable amount of sand in the process.

(plant eaters) and live by nibbling away at grass and plant stems and roots of various kinds.

The shrews (Soricidae) are insectivores (insect eaters) and spend most of their life in search of insects among the grass and leaf litter. Their sole aim in life seems to be to eat as much as possible, as quickly as possible, then rest a short while before repeating the action. You may not see them but you may well hear their tiny squeaks as one shrew meets another. They are quarrelsome little animals and make a great deal of fuss when they happen to meet.

### Long-tailed fieldmouse
In the undergrowth of seaside hedges lives another small mammal – the long-tailed fieldmouse (*Apodemus sylvaticus*). It is a delightful little animal but almost entirely nocturnal as you can see by its large light-collecting night eyes, sensitive whiskers and huge ears which it moves like radar dishes.

### Mole
Many crop fields stretch down to the top of beaches and both there and in rough grass of all kinds you will find signs of the mole (*Talpa europaea*). Those familiar hummocks are the waste earth produced as it burrows for worms. Early summer is the best time to spot one, for then the youngsters seem more inclined to come above ground, but it is a rare sighting and one to be remembered.

### Kestrel
Naturally enough, all these small

mammals attract the attention of predators like the kestrel (*Falco tinnunculus*) and you will often see one or a pair of these birds hovering on the updraughts and searching the grass below. If you sit and watch you will almost certainly see one dive down to seize its prey, although you seldom see the prey itself. In midsummer you may hear their young calling when they first leave the nest which is built into the face of the cliff.

### Peregrine falcon

Where there are tall cliffs well away from people you may be able to watch the peregrine falcon (*Falco peregrinus*), now sadly a rare species in so many of its former habitats. The male, known as a tiercel, is much smaller than the female, referred to as a falcon, but both are marvellous fliers. To see one stoop from near the clouds right down to sea level is a never to be forgotten sight. Their food, naturally enough, is mainly those birds that share its habitat: gulls, waders, jackdaws, pigeons and stock doves.

They frequently hunt over estuaries but, in spite of their speed, are not always successful in catching their prey. By keeping low, twisting and turning prey often outwit their breathtaking rushes.

### Insects

If you can find a hollow, sheltered from the wind, or a piece of land protected by hedges, you will be surprised to discover how many insects have gathered there.

Butterflies, for instance, are often quite abundant in such places whereas on open coastlines you may see very few. June is the ideal time to see them, but the species vary in number and kind according to the area.

If you are very fortunate you may come upon a butterfly migration. I remember one occasion when exploring the sloping hills above a shingle beach. We were photographing the bee orchids (*Ophrys apifera*) that grew there, when quite suddenly it 'snowed' butterflies. Hundreds of them fluttered down and landed, apparently exhausted, among the flowers. They were clouded yellow butterflies (*Colias crocea*). We were in Dorset, England, and they had probably come from France, so they had flown a very considerable distance over the English Channel.

Three species are particularly common in rough meadows and downland that are often found close to the sea. They are the common blue (*Polyomotus icarus*), small copper (*Lycaena phlaeas*) and the small skipper (*Thymelicus sylvestris*). Because the landforms along the coast are so variable, many of the common inland butterflies will be found.

**Butterfly watching** It is quite easy to approach butterflies. Move very slowly and smoothly because any sudden movement sets them into flight. The best way to watch them is to sit near a well massed group of flowers and wait for the butterflies to come to you. Try and choose a warm, sunny and windless day, for then butterflies fly more freely and are much easier to see. On windy days they tend to cling to flowerheads or fly close to the ground.

You may find difficulty in sorting out the coastal butterflies from moths, and although it is often stated in books that butterflies fly by day whereas moths by night, there are some moths that are diurnal (active during the day). The surest way to tell the difference is to look at the antennae. If they are clubbed at the ends then you are looking at a butterfly. If they are any other shape you are looking at a moth.

**Moths on the wing** One moth you will see flying very fast in long, straight lines is the oak eggar (*Lasiocampa quercus*). It is light brown in colour and lays its eggs on clover (*Trifolium* spp), thrift (*Armeria maritima*) and other coastal plants. Its larvae are large, velvety black with white lines, and have some stiff hairs sticking up from the back. Look for them among the grasses from early spring to June. The adult moth flies during August and September.

The drinker moth (*Philudoria potatoria*) is also to be found along the coast although, like most insects, it does occur elsewhere. The adult is rather like the oak eggar. The large larvae feed on grasses from August to October and then some of them go into hibernation to emerge once more in the following April. It is then, when there is dew or rain upon the grasses, that it has been seen to 'drink' – hence the popular name.

Moth and butterfly antennae

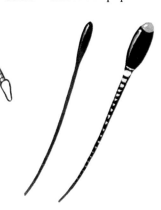

moths have jointed antennae of various shapes

butterflies have antennae with club-shaped ends

## Exploring sand dunes

At first sight, sand dunes may look static and rather dull, but I think you might be quite surprised to discover how lively they are.

At its simplest, a dune is a large area of sand. Two things are needed to build one: a plentiful supply of sand and a great deal of wind. It has been calculated that a minimum wind speed of 16 kph is required to move sand grains.

Wind and sun together dry the beaches, and if the wind is strong enough it will then blow the grains of sand along. If you look along a beach in the right weather, you will see a misty movement just above and along the surface. The beach is actually moving!

Any small obstruction in its way will momentarily halt this flow of sand and it will begin to build up. If you look at a piece of stranded seaweed at the top of the beach when the wind is blowing, you will see this happening as sand grains fill in the spaces among the seaweed. Slowly the weed disappears as a small sand dune forms on the sheltered side. Even more slowly it can be seen to be growing – or moving – landwards.

On the Atlantic coast of France, the winds blowing in from the Atlantic have built up the largest dunes in Europe. They are moving inland like a vast bulldozer, covering even the tallest pine trees that grow there.

In order to live in the moving sand of dunes, animals and plants have to be well adapted.

Marram grass helps to anchor sand dunes. Unfortunately it is easily eroded away by human feet.

## Plant life

When you walk along the top of the beach, where the dunes begin, you will see some plants growing, and a few of them are even among the seaweed on the strandline. Two of these are likely to be sea rocket (*Cakile maritima*) and sea sandwort (*Honkenya peploides*). A grass known as sand couch (*Agropyron juncei-forme*) will also be found here. These three plants are able to live in this rather hostile place, because they grow faster than the sand can increase in depth.

We usually think of plants as static things, unable to move, except for occasionally swaying or bending. Yet, these maritime plants have to move in order to survive. In fact, a growing dune system is a kind of battleground, where plants are always trying to establish a bridgehead.

Sand couch sends out a network of underground stems through the moving sand, and in this way, anchors itself. At the same time, it grows and sends up shoots and leaves which trap the wind blown sand, causing it to fall to the base of the plant, and so begin to form a dune. Often in storms, the sea sweeps over the plants, washing some of the sand away and exposing many of the underground stems. Yet, still they survive and grow in salty, moving sand.

Once sand couch is well established, another plant moves in. This is marram grass (*Ammophila arenaria*).

It's really an amazing plant, for it grows in places where sand is deepening at nearly 1 metre in a year. It has both horizontal and vertical roots, and so captures the sand, and begins to grow all over it. Thus, a single marram plant may cover an entire dune by producing more and more plants, each connected to the other by a network of buried stems.

When this has happened, the dune becomes fairly stationary and other plants are able to grow, such as sea holly (*Eryngium maritimum*) with its spiky, shiny leaves. It has roots that go more than 2 metres straight down into the sand, searching for freshwater and food as well as providing anchorage. Once this happens, the dune moves less and less, and other plants arrive and slowly become established. Among these will be a sea bindweed (*Calystegia soldanella*) and sea spurges (*Euphorbia* spp).

## Animal life

Once there are flowers growing on the dune, insects will arrive to feed on the nectar and foliage. Some very obvious ones will be the larvae of the cinnabar moth (*Callimorpha jacobaeae*), and you will find these orange and black striped larvae feeding on the ragworts (*Senecio* spp).

Grayling butterflies (*Satyrus semele*) are common on many dune systems, although when at rest, they merge perfectly with the surrounding sand. They are on the wing in

129

July and August and you may be fortunate to see their courtship display, as the male performs its dance to the female.

Grasshoppers (Orthoptera) of many species will be found leaping among the burnet rose (*Rosa pimpinellifolia*), a rose bush which spreads its branches low to the ground among the brambles, growing out over the dunes.

Very steadily, the number of plant and animal species increase and then eventually, larger mammals from fieldmouse to fox move in. On well established dunes, you can start finding out a little about their way of life, by searching for and studying their tracks and signs.

## Tracks

A particularly good area to begin tracking is along the seaward side of dunes on the edge of the tide line. It is here that seabirds and waders walk in search of food. Basically, the signs will be their footprints, and a very great deal can be discovered by a close study of these.

On many beaches, you will see the footprints of oystercatchers. Follow them along, and you will begin to notice that about every six or so footsteps, there is a neat hole on one or other side of the tracks. Bend down, and look closely at these holes. You will find that some are, in fact, two holes, separated by a thin sand wall.

Why not try digging out a few of both kinds of hole with your finger? As you do this, you will certainly reveal a sandhopper. Many of these small holes, then, are made by the sandhoppers, and from this, it is but a small step to assume that the larger holes are where the oystercatcher probed down with its beak – to catch a sandhopper. Later, you might like to confirm that oystercatchers do, in fact, bore into the sand in this way, by watching them with a pair of binoculars.

It is by clever detection work like this that you will discover all kinds of facts about animals, and their ways of life.

On the ridged and patterned sand surface of dunes, there may be groups of footprints in fours. By the size and pattern, you will soon come to recognize them as those of the rabbit. On occasion, you will find their tracks leading right down to the edge of the sea. What they find of interest there is a mystery, but maybe they too, like to explore this small extension of their territory.

Hedgehogs (*Erinaceus europaeus*) live among the dunes in some localities, and their tracks have regular paw marks, although when they are scenting around for food, they often leave the marks of their spines on the sand – long surface scratches among the footprints.

If you search carefully in slightly damp sand at the edges of a clump of marram, you may come across the tracks of a fieldmouse. They are distinguishable by their tiny size.

One unusual track, although common on some dunes, looks as if a length of chain, with links about 3 millimetres long and 2 millimetres wide, had been laid on the sand. It's the track of an insect, one of the many species of beetle or weevil that inhabits such places. Identifying it as the sign of an insect, is about as close as you can expect to get, unless you are fortunate enough to see the little creature.

Fox tracks and dog tracks can easily be confused, and the latter are of course very common on dune systems. In general, the fox travels in a fairly purposeful way, and its tracks are therefore in straight lines, whereas those of the dog wander here, there and everywhere.

The footprints of a fox are neat and narrow, with the claw marks usually visible. With a little experience, you will also come to recognize the scent left by this mammal. Its strong, musty scent lasts for several hours after it has passed by.

I once came upon the signs of a fox feeding. To begin with, I was following the tracks of a natterjack toad (*Bufo calamita*) from the small depression in which it had spent the day. The tracks led for some 30 metres, and then I noticed those of a fox converging on to them. For a further 30 metres, the fox tracks joined those of the toad. The fox obviously was following the toad's scent trail. Then finally, there were the marks of the fox springing, and the toad's footprints ended in some disturbed sand.

**Photographing tracks** The best photographs of tracks are to be taken in the very early morning, when the sun is low and casting long shadows. Just after dawn, the tracks are fresh and have not yet been kicked away by the seashore visitors. Although the evening sun also casts long shadows, the tracks themselves will be rather tatty and lack the clear, crisp outline you can see in the early morning.

Search carefully before you take a picture. Select those tracks which look attractive and are typical of the animal, and it often makes a more appealing picture if you choose a viewpoint, so that the line of the tracks goes diagonally across the picture.

Tracks of a hedgehog and rabbit. Unusual scratch marks made by the hedgehog's spines can be seen.

**Drawing and recording tracks by plaster casts** Simple sketches of tracks help to form a record of what you have seen. If you enjoy drawing, why not take a pencil and sketch book with you next time you visit some dunes? If you want to be fairly scientific, then you should measure the prints, and enter these figures on your sketch.

But undoubtedly, the most interesting way to record tracks and footprints is to make plaster casts.

The equipment needed is simple. You will need: about 3 kilos of plaster of Paris (bought at a local chemist); a small container in which to mix it; a bottle of water; a stick for stirring.

Before going out, cut some rings from a detergent container or corn-flake packet, and by cutting them from different sized packets, you will have a good variety of rings. Each ring should be about 7 centimetres deep.

Having arrived on the dunes, seashore or estuary, look around for a damp area – especially if it's sandy. Choose a good, plain and firm set of footprints, and push a

**Making a plaster cast**

1. Choose a suitable print or prints.
2. Push a ring of card ⅓ of its depth into the sand around the print.
3. Pour in plaster and leave to harden.
4. Remove card and clean the underside of the cast.

Equipment you will need

suitably-sized card ring into the ground around them. About a third of the depth of the ring should be in the ground. Next, you will have to mix the plaster. Pour about four cupfuls of water into the mixing container, and begin to add the plaster. Do this a little at a time, and keep the solution well stirred. Add just enough plaster to make the solution a little less than creamy, so that it will pour easily.

Pour the plaster of Paris into the ring, but make sure you do not pour it directly on to the actual footprints, because this spoils their outline. Simply allow the solution to pour on to the sand between the footprints, so that it flows gently into them. If you have gauged the amount closely, you should finish up with a depth of about 3 to 4 centimetres of plaster covering the prints.

All you have to do now is wait for the plaster to harden. This may take up to 10 minutes, but it is better to leave it much longer, so that it goes quite firm. While you are waiting, you can take some more casts.

When the plaster is hard, very gently prise up the ring of card, and lift the cast out of the sand. The underside, where the footprints are, will be covered by sand, so place it carefully in the bucket together with any other plaster casts you have made.

At home, carefully tear away the card surround, and wash off the sand. The cast can now be left to dry. Painting is a matter of choice, but it is a good idea to write all the necessary details on the back, before you forget them.

## Bird pellets

Any birds that eat other creatures have to rid themselves of the bones. This is usually done by the predator regurgitating the bones in the form of a pellet. Owls and hawks produce pellets in which the bones are well wrapped in an outer coat of fur from their prey.

Seabirds, however, feed largely on creatures without fur and hair, and their pellets are not as stable as those of owls. Whereas an owl pellet may remain on the floor of a barn for a very long time, the pellet of a herring gull (*Larus argentatus*) begins to break up as soon as it falls.

The best place to look for such pellets is along the beach, dunes or rocks where seabirds have roosted. All you will find will be a small pile of bones the size of a cherry. If you can identify these bones, you will discover a little more about the food of that particular bird.

However, sorting out the exact identity of a fish from its bones is really the job for a scientist, so you may have to be satisfied in simply arranging them on a card. Clean them first by treating them in bleach as described in the chapter on seashells. Occasionally great black-backed gulls (*Larus marinus*) do eat small mammals, but you should easily be able to distinguish between mammal and fish bones.

Here is a selection of animals and their signs, and plants that live at the edge of the sea.

# The land margins

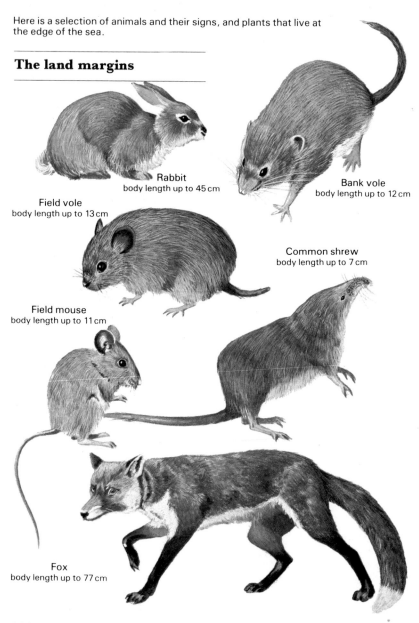

Rabbit
body length up to 45 cm

Bank vole
body length up to 12 cm

Field vole
body length up to 13 cm

Common shrew
body length up to 7 cm

Field mouse
body length up to 11 cm

Fox
body length up to 77 cm

Brown rat
body length up to 27 cm

Mink
body length up to 37 cm

Kestrel (male)
length up to 34 cm

Peregrine falcon
length up to 50 cm

Mole
body length up to 15 cm

Hedgehog
body length up to 27 cm

Clouded yellow (female)
wingspan up to 5.8 cm

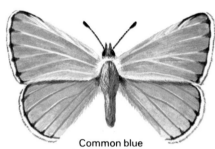
Common blue
wingspan up to 3.6 cm

Small skipper
wingspan up to 3 cm

Small copper
wingspan up to 3 cm

Drinker moth
wingspan up to 6 cm

Oak eggar
wingspan up to 5.5 cm

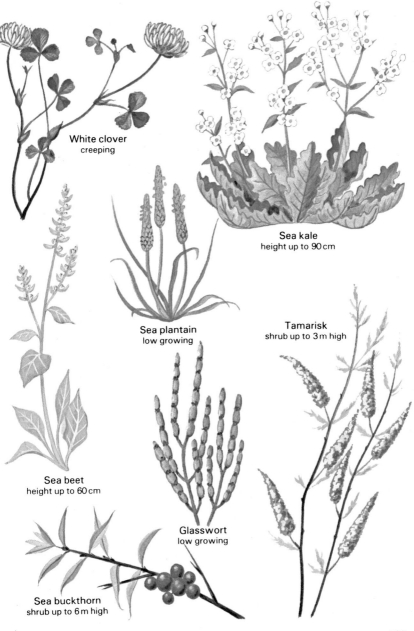

White clover
creeping

Sea kale
height up to 90 cm

Sea plantain
low growing

Tamarisk
shrub up to 3 m high

Sea beet
height up to 60 cm

Glasswort
low growing

Sea buckthorn
shrub up to 6 m high

137

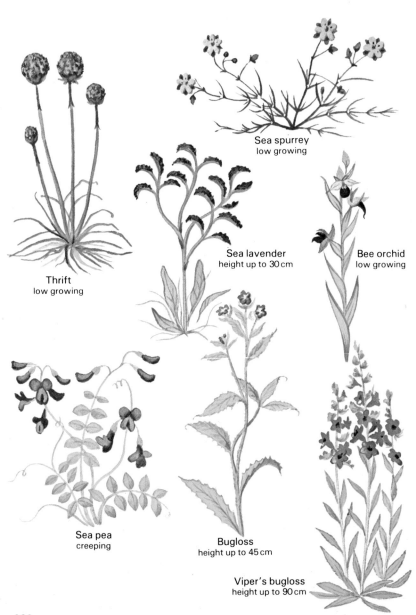

Sea spurrey
low growing

Thrift
low growing

Sea lavender
height up to 30 cm

Bee orchid
low growing

Sea pea
creeping

Bugloss
height up to 45 cm

Viper's bugloss
height up to 90 cm

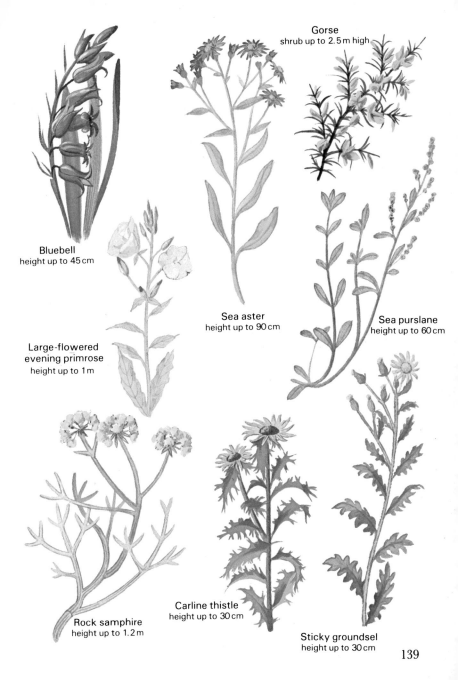

Bluebell
height up to 45 cm

Gorse
shrub up to 2.5 m high

Large-flowered
evening primrose
height up to 1 m

Sea aster
height up to 90 cm

Sea purslane
height up to 60 cm

Rock samphire
height up to 1.2 m

Carline thistle
height up to 30 cm

Sticky groundsel
height up to 30 cm

139

# Sand dunes

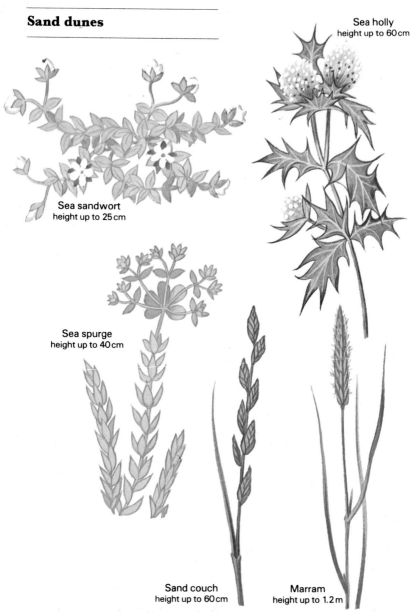

Sea holly
height up to 60 cm

Sea sandwort
height up to 25 cm

Sea spurge
height up to 40 cm

Sand couch
height up to 60 cm

Marram
height up to 1.2 m

140

Sea rocket
height up to 45 cm

Burnet rose
height up to 1 m

Sea bindweed
low growing

Cinnabar moth
wingspan up to 4.5 cm

Grayling butterfly
wingspan up to 5 cm

# TRACKS

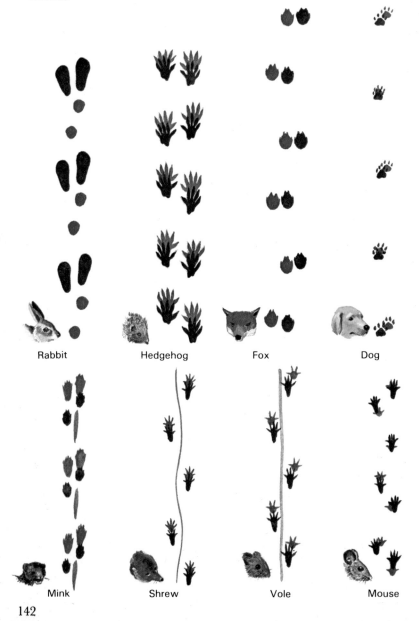

Rabbit

Hedgehog

Fox

Dog

Mink

Shrew

Vole

Mouse

142

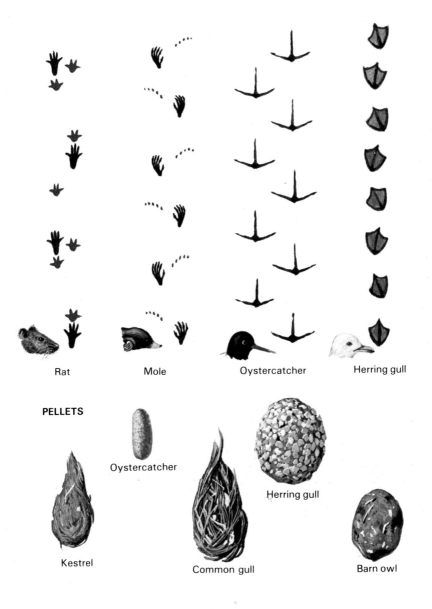

Rat

Mole

Oystercatcher

Herring gull

**PELLETS**

Oystercatcher

Kestrel

Herring gull

Common gull

Barn owl

143

# Changing shores

## After dark

At night you will discover a variety of animals that you would not see during the hours of daylight. The reason they are easier to find is simply that the daytime predators, such as flocks of seabirds, have left the shore. The seashore creatures seem to know this and move about much more freely.

Before setting out on a night search you will need a good source of light. Torches are fine providing they are powerful and project a

The seashore is always changing. After dark many seashore animals such as prawns, shrimps, crabs and small fish move about much more freely. An hour after sunset is a good time to begin exploration, providing the tide is low.

medium wide beam. Spot lights are rather limiting since they cover such a small area. Equally useless are very small hand torches.

If you are going to make a number of visits you might consider buying a Tilley lamp. This is a paraffin pressure light and provides marvellous source of illumination. Do not use the types that have separate pressure tanks, as these are not intended for out-of-door use and are not wind resistant.

Remember to check the time of low tide. This is most important at night when visibility is limited, and a rising tide can maroon you in an awkward and sometimes dangerous situation. Finally take a friend with you, preferably a local naturalist who knows the shore and understands the tides.

## A sandy shore

If you walk towards the tide's edge on a sandy beach about an hour before low tide, you may see the sudden flash of silver of sand-eels.

There are two species – the greater sand-eel (*Hyperoplus lanceolatus*) which grows up to 200 millimetres long, and the lesser sand-eel (*Ammodytes tobianus*) which grows to 100 millimetres long. Both spend their time swimming in shoals, or burrowing into the sand near low tide mark.

When your light reveals one, watch it and see how it burrows into the sand like a flexible silver shaft. Their tapered bodies are covered with tiny scales which protect them as they move through the sand, which they do at a quite remarkable speed. If you scrape with your finger or a piece of wood and disturb the sand where the eel disappeared you may cause it to jump out of the sand again, so that you will be able to watch it for a little longer.

If you are lucky, you may come upon immense shoals of sand-eels in the shallows at the edge of the sea. June, July and August are the best times for these silver tides when mackerel (*Scomber* spp) sometimes chase the sand-eels on to the beach. Providing you visit the shore often enough, you will have a lucky night when the sand-eels are flashing in the moonlight.

On many sandy shores you will encounter the masked crab (*Corystes cassivelaunus*). It is a species that is

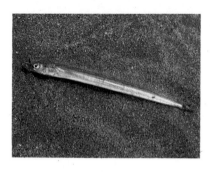

As the tide ebbs, a few sand-eels get stranded. However, they often burrow into the sand.

very particular about the grain size of the sand and therefore tends to be rather local in its distribution. You will see why this is so as you read on.

The best time of year to search for them is May, June, and July, near low spring tide on beaches where low tide occurs after dark.

During the hours of daylight masked crabs remain buried beneath the sand, safe from the searching and hungry herring gulls, but after dark, when the birds are roosting, the crabs come to the surface and crawl about over the sand.

One reason why it is particularly good to search in early summer, is that then, in many places, these crabs gather together in mating assemblies. They come inshore from deeper water and find one another in the darkness. As you search you will find occasional pairs with the male holding a female in his large pincer claw and often he holds her above his head.

You will see why it is called a masked crab if you look at its back. There you will see the shape of a face and the general shape of its back also tends to accentuate the image.

As you bring your lamp closer to one of these crabs it will begin to burrow down away from the light. It does this by pushing the sand away from its body with its front legs, and pulling itself down into the sand with its rear legs. Then when it is almost buried you will notice that its antennae stretch upwards out of the sand – the only sign that a masked crab is there.

Use a hand lens to look really closely at these antennae and you will discover how the masked crab is able to breathe whilst surrounded by sand. You will see that there are two of these antennae and that each has a double row of stiff hairs facing inwards. When the two antennae are brought together, these hairs interlock to form a fine network tube. This enables water to be drawn in and down for breathing, whilst preventing sand grains clogging the breathing apparatus. It's a simple but very effective filter system.

Males are easy to tell from females because male masked crabs have enormously long pincer claws whereas the females' claws are quite short.

You will probably find one or two sand-burrowing starfish on the surface too. A short and rather scratchy track shows where they have been moving. Sometimes when

Four stages of a masked crab burrowing.

you bring your light close to them, they begin to sink slowly down into the sand and finally disappear from sight, leaving a vague starfish-shaped depression in the soft sand.

On beaches where razor shells are common you may be fortunate to find one sticking up out of its burrow. Seize it and see if you can pull it out. You may be surprised to discover how strongly it tries to resist by pulling itself down again. If you succeed in withdrawing it, replace the tip of its large white foot in the top of its burrow and watch as it quickly re-buries itself.

Look out too for cockles somersaulting their way along the edge of the tide, and as you wade into the sea you will almost certainly see small hermit crabs scuttling away from your light beam.

On the light-dappled sand below the water, you will perhaps see small flatfish darting away, disturbed by your feet. Crabs of many kinds will be running sideways away from your light. If the sand is near rocks, there will certainly be green shore crabs about and an occasional swimming crab.

If the sandy shore has a margin against a pier or a jetty wall, spend a while searching there. You may come upon some common starfish and if the situation is right you will find dahlia anemones opening far wider than they ever do by day. They like the cracks in such structures so you will have to search carefully.

Above all, remember that there are no *certain* places where a particular animal will be seen. There is always a surprise awaiting you, and it is after dark when the best specimens reveal themselves. It takes both time and experience to get to know the best places and the best time of year, but acquiring that knowledge is perhaps the best part of being a naturalist.

## A rocky shore

It is a tricky business walking over weed-slippery rocks with only a small circle of light to help you, and all too easy to step on to seaweed floating on a rock pool and fill your waders with cold seawater. Step carefully, and remember some of those pools are quite deep.

It's quiet on the shore at night, and if you listen you will hear the occasional tiny rattle as a periwinkle or dogwhelk drops from an overhanging rock ledge into the water.

Move slowly and quietly up to a pool and rest your lamp on the seaweed. You may see the eyes of a prawn as the animal moves over the bottom. Nearby may be seen a green shore crab busily eating something it has found and which was left behind by the ebb tide.

Blennies and gobies come out from hiding after dark, and swim quietly in the open spaces of rock pools. If you happen to make a sudden movement or let a shadow fall upon the water, they will be

At night, limpets crawl over algae-covered rock surfaces and browse. Their peculiar zig-zag track can be seen on rocks when the tide is out.

gone in a flash. They do not believe in taking chances. Sea scorpions also leave their weedy hide-outs, no doubt to go in search of food.

In the deeper pools where a tidal current is running, you often find 20 or more prawns hanging on to the seaweed fronds, head into current, motionless except for the swaying of the seaweed.

Because it is dark and the air is cool and damp, limpets exposed on the rock surfaces frequently move. This is something you seldom see in daylight. In the pools they will be browsing, along with periwinkles.

If you take a few pieces of fish along with you and drop these into a pool, all sorts of mini-struggles will begin. A prawn may home in and

begin to feed, only to be disturbed by a crab seizing on to the food and driving the prawn off, and then a scorpion fish settling the matter by swallowing the food in one great gulp.

There are the unexpected discoveries too. A stranded jellyfish, a giant spider crab creaking its way into hiding as you approach, a guillemot resting on a rock, a shoal of baby mullet, even a heron feeding on sand-eels.

Search the promenade wall, slipway or steps close to the beach. Move your light slowly and search carefully, and you will find the sea-slater (*Ligia oceanica*). It is quite large – about 25 millimetres long, and looks rather like an overgrown

After dark the sea-slater crawls around damp rock faces and harbour walls.

woodlouse. It is in fact related to the woodlouse found in our gardens and countryside.

It only comes out after dark, and spends the day hiding beneath rocks or in crevices and cracks. Its favourite food is seaweed and it goes down to the beach to browse along the strandline, although it will also eat dead animals.

Sea-slaters have seven pairs of legs, and if you try to catch one of these animals you will quickly discover how fast they can run. They can rush up a vertical surface and disappear into a small crack in a matter of seconds.

Their colour blends so well with their surroundings, that when motionless, they merge completely. No doubt this camouflage helps them to survive should they ever be disturbed and out in daylight.

# Different seasons

## Seasons in the sea

When we look at that great expanse of water we call the sea, it is not immediately obvious that each year it is producing a vast harvest of plant and animal life.

Yet in the sea, beneath every acre of surface water, nearly 6 tonnes of plant life are produced each year. Since most of these plants are microscopic in size you will appreciate that their total number is quite astronomical!

The annual story of this great cycle of life in the sea is a fascinating one and you can best begin its study in January.

**Winter** In January the amount of sunlight shining on the sea is small, and just as on land growth ceases at that time of year, the same thing happens in the sea. Without sunlight, green plants cannot grow.

So it is in winter that, apart from the larger animals, the sea is comparitively clear of plankton. Furthermore, with the death and decay of many plants and animals, large quantities of minerals (chemicals) are being released back into the sea and the 'salt' is becoming more concentrated.

Towards the end of December and into January, the few early spawning animals are giving out their eggs and larvae which begin to drift in the surface waters and populate them.

**Spring** With the approach of March, the sun rises higher and the sunlight becomes brighter and there is a sudden outburst of plant growth.

The microscopic plants responsible for this massive flowering are called diatoms. They are single celled algae which somewhat resemble microscopic plastic boxes.

When the time comes for them to reproduce, they simply split in two and their rate of increase is so vast that in a few days their numbers have increased a hundred-fold.

If you want to see these tiny diatoms you will need to either make or buy a plankton tow net.

The material must be very tightly meshed. Open network such as that used in nylon curtains is far too wide a mesh and the little plants will simply drift out of the net as fast as they flow in. Bolting cloth or a good quality muslin are quite suitable. The purpose of the jar at the end of the net is simply to act as a reservoir into which the diatoms finally flow after passing down the length of the net.

The net should be towed VERY SLOWLY (slow walking pace) behind a boat or dropped into the sea from a pier or jetty and gently and slowly drawn through the water. After about five minutes, draw the net in, and transfer the water from the reservoir jar to a plastic bucket.

Usually you will see very little,

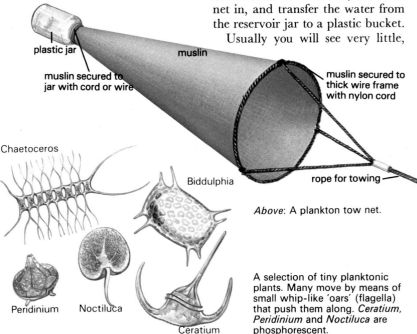

plastic jar

muslin secured to jar with cord or wire

muslin

muslin secured to thick wire frame with nylon cord

rope for towing

*Above*: A plankton tow net.

Chaetoceros

Biddulphia

Peridinium   Noctiluca

Ceratium

A selection of tiny planktonic plants. Many move by means of small whip-like 'oars' (flagella) that push them along. *Ceratium*, *Peridinium* and *Noctiluca* are phosphorescent.

151

for remember most of these plants you are trying to net are microscopic in size. Some may be nearly a millimetre across but most are less than .0001 millimetres.

You will need a microscope to see them properly as hand lenses are not powerful enough. Perhaps you could take your catch along to school and use one of their microscopes, or else try to contact someone at your local museum or a local naturalist and persuade him to let you use his.

Use a pipette to draw up a few drops of water from the bottom of the bucket and place them on a slide. With a low power lens you will be able to see your first diatoms, and then perhaps use a higher power to magnify the detail of a few.

Suddenly as you look through the microscope a whole new world will open up. A world of strangely semi-transparent shapes glittering and sparkling and full of amber coloured spots. Some are joined together to form chains, some lie side by side like matches in a box, a few have thin strands spreading outwards like hairs, whilst others are single, simple crystal boxes. But all are beautiful.

**Summer** The great increase in plant growth provides ideal conditions for the incredible number of animals that now arrive in the plankton 'meadows'. The young stages of starfish, sea urchins and worms join with shellfish larvae and countless others as the adult animals

spawn. From March onwards, for instance, every seashore barnacle pours its life into the sea and at that time of the year their larvae are one of the commonest inshore plankton animals. Fish, too, are releasing millions upon millions of eggs and it is not surprising that immense numbers of baby fish are soon swimming through the plankton 'meadows' and feeding on the diatoms.

But all this wealth of life and feasting has one result: the meadows of diatoms begin to decrease as they

fulfil their function of providing food for the animals. Another factor leading to this decline in diatoms is the dwindling amount of minerals on which they have been feeding. They have quite literally used up all the available food.

The growing fish then feed on the other growing animals, and the general size of the plankton species increases.

On a winter beach the snow holds tracks and signs of seabirds and other animals. Each has a story to tell, but a rising tide melts them all away.

**Autumn** After midsummer the peak populations dwindle, but when the first October gales come, the minerals that have been 'locked up' in the deeper water are stirred up. This results in a second blooming of the sea meadows, although it is considerably smaller than the springtime one.

By midwinter, the seas are at their barest, because the sun declines and with it the number of diatoms.

### Seasons on the shore
**Winter** If you visit the beach regularly through the year you will soon begin to recognize seasonal differences. A good time to start is in winter, when it is cold on the shore, and sometimes ice covers the surface of the pools and sunlight is at its minimum.

One of the shore animals quick to react to these conditions is the prawn which migrates out into deeper and less cold water. Snakelocks anemones become smaller and smaller as the green algae that live within their bodies decrease due to the failing sunshine. By January, these anemones may be cherry-sized, whereas only a few months previously they were as large as your hand.

You will almost certainly notice that most of the female green shore crabs are carrying eggs during the winter months. You can tell if the eggs are freshly laid for they will be a bright orange colour. As time passes, they change to dull brown and finally

153

a mid-grey. This final colour stage is reached in late May or early June, when the larvae finally emerge.

In general, the winter months are quiet on the shore and the pools rather bare, although blennies and gobies are still to be found. The male of the latter may well be in its dark breeding colours.

By late February, you will see black-headed gulls (*Larus ridibundus*) in both winter and summer plumage, for a few will still have white heads with a dark eye spot although others are growing their chocolate-brown summer headdress. Also the herring gulls (*Larus argentatus*) are beginning to get together in pairs.

**Spring** Spring on the shore begins with the coming of April and soon there is a great upsurge of life. I always feel that the first sign of the new season is the discovery of the white, spirally coiled egg ribbons of the sea-lemon (*Archidoris pseudoargus*). They are quite beautiful as they gleam on the rock surfaces, and if you examine them closely with a hand lens you will be able to see the hundreds of tiny eggs that will soon become sea-slugs. Finding the adult sea-lemon is quite another matter. It is superbly camouflaged to blend exactly with the sponges and encrustations on the rocks where it crawls slowly about, after its arrival from deeper water.

Springtime, you see, is the time when the urge to spawn brings many animals on to the shore, where they are not normally found. One such animal is the small sea-slug (*Onchidoris fusca*) which in some seasons, on shores that it favours, may be found in very large numbers almost covering the rocks around the margin of low water neap tides. At such times, it is a difficult business sorting out the slugs from their eggs and slime, but you can count yourself fortunate to see such a gathering.

The grey sea-slug (*Aeolidia papillosa*) will also be found in the springtime, for it too comes ashore to spawn. It is a handsome slug up to 7 centimetres in length, and its back is adorned with a mat of soft projections. Search for it beneath large rocks, but do not be deceived by its appearance, for when retracted it looks very much like a snakelocks anemone. Incidentally, anemones are its main food.

One inshore migration that is quite spectacular is the arrival of another sea-slug, the sea-hare (*Aplysia punctata*), to lay its eggs. You can never be sure that they will come each year. There is often a run of a year or more when they do not come. Then, for no obvious reason, the next year you find them once again.

To find them you will have to search from the middle shore down to low water springs on flat rocky platforms well covered with seaweeds. I have noticed that they are frequently to be found among red seaweeds such as caragheen or Irish moss. It is also often found feeding on the green sea-lettuce.

Sea-hares are not easy to spot unless they are moving, because their deep brownish-green coloration stippled with yellowish streaks matches so perfectly the seaweed covered rocks. When at rest they contract into 3 centimetre long blobs that closely resemble beadlet anemones.

When you pick one up do not be surprised to find that your fingers have gone a deep purple colour, for when disturbed, sea-hares release a cloud of liquid which turns the sea-water bright purple.

Sea-hares lay their eggs on stones, rocks or among seaweed. They are salmon-coloured gelatinous strings and easily recognized. In fact it is much easier to find the spawn than it is to find the slugs. Like most sea-slugs, they die shortly after spawning so their inshore migration is a one-way journey.

You will come upon eggs of many kinds as you search the shore, and both in winter and spring look out for a spawning gathering of dog whelks. Such gatherings consist of about a dozen or more dogwhelks, close together, and amongst them will be seen their whitish-yellow, vase-shaped egg capsules. Take a closer look at one of them. If you snip off the top end of the capsule and gently squeeze it, you will see the eggs ooze out. There may be as many as 500 in each capsule, but only about 6 will ever develop into adult dogwhelks. The remainder are nurse eggs whose sole purpose is to be eaten by the first embryos to hatch. Look for these eggs beneath rocky overhangs and in crevices well down the middle shore. Harbour walls, jetties and concrete piers are also good places to search at low tide during the springtime, because

The strange beauty of the world of plankton is shown by this larva of a hermit crab. Stalked eyes help it to find prey, and to see predators.

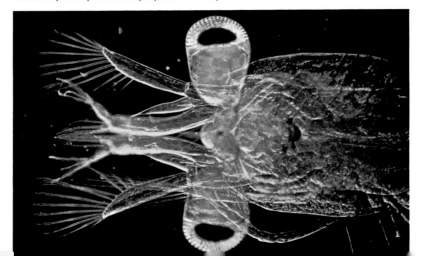

The dogwhelk lays its egg capsules near to its main food: acorn barnacles or mussels. After about four months, ten or more shelled young emerge from each capsule.

their large flat surfaces offer an ideal habitat for many of these early visitors to the shore.

As you walk about the shore at this time of the year you will probably discover small blobs of green translucent jelly, loosely adhering to the wracks. They are a little larger than a pea and are the egg masses of the green worm, *Eulalia viridis*, which grows to about 7 centimetres in length and will be found crawling around in the wracks as the tide ebbs.

**Summer** In summer you will almost certainly find pipefishes among the seaweeds on the lower shore especially where the weeds are growing in pools. If you find one, look carefully at its underside, and if your specimen happens to be a male you will notice that its belly is stretched into two swollen ridges. Within these, are the developing eggs. Male pipefishes pick up the eggs after the female has laid them, and carry them until they hatch.

Early summer is the time to search for the nest of the ballan wrasse (*Labrus bergylta*). It takes some skill and patience to find a nest of one of these fish, because they are rather roughly made from pieces of seaweed. Look for these nests under rocky overhangs which are constricted by boulders or large stones, and there, among the sparse seaweed, you may spot the nest. It is about the size of a large grapefruit and looks very untidy and rather as if some stray seaweed has drifted into the cracks between rocks. If you examine the mass carefully you will discover the eggs spread throughout the nest, although the more solid mass of eggs is usually in the centre. Be very careful not to damage the nest and try to content yourself with merely taking a look.

It would appear that wrasse build their nests when the tide is well up the shore and probably return on each rising tide to complete the job. Since spring tides usually leave the nests out of water, the fish are unable to guard them, unless perhaps they return with the flood tide.

Female blennies lay their eggs in crannies in the rocks. They lay up to 400 and then abandon them to the males who remain on guard until they hatch. Compared to the vast number of eggs produced by a cod, this is very few, but since the eggs are guarded there is no need to produce so many.

In early summer you may see a butterfish guarding its egg ball. There is usually a pair and they seem to share the duty. Eggs are often to be found in shells such as scallops or very large cockles.

On both the sandy shore and in rock pools with fine sandy bottoms, the common goby (*Gobius minutus*) lays its eggs. You will have to search most carefully by watching such pools for the movement of one of these little fish. If you see one gently fanning with its fins close to an up-turned shell and making sudden darts at any intruder venturing too close, you can be sure it has some eggs beneath that shell. The male is, for his small size, a fierce guard and shows great care and devotion to the eggs.

Early summer sees the return of the prawns from their winter hideaway in deeper water. They come inshore and the males begin to cast their shells. After a few weeks they are hard again, having 'grown' in the interval. Now the females cast their skins and whilst they are in this soft condition, pairing takes place.

The male places his sperms on her underside and almost immediately she releases her eggs and wafts them backwards and sticks them on to her swimming tufts. To do this, a special cement runs out from this part of her body and so completely covers the eggs that it binds them into place.

Most of the female prawns you find in midsummer will have this dark egg mass on their undersides, and very soon after that, each will lay at least 1500 eggs. A few weeks later, the larval prawns break free from the egg cases and swim into the already dwindling plankton.

A very exciting summer find, but very rare, is an octopus. There are two species: the common octopus (*Octopus vulgaris*) with a double line of suckers along its tentacles and the lesser or curled octopus (*Eledone cirrhosa*) which has a single line of suckers.

A common octopus in an aquarium showing two lines of suckers on its tentacles.
*Inset*: The tentacles of a common octopus and a lesser or curled octopus.

Octopuses are delightful animals with a straight-forward intelligence that makes them most attractive. The stories of giant octopuses dragging people underwater are simply nonsense, for these animals are most shy and retiring.

Should you come upon one you will be amazed to see how it changes colour. Wave after wave of colours spread across its body, and the more excited it becomes, the more rapid the colour change.

Handling an octopus is a difficult business. It has eight tentacles and since you have only two arms, all sorts of problems arise. One part of its body to avoid is the mouth. It's in the form of a beak and situated in the central meeting place of its eight tentacles. It can cut through your skin and give you quite a pinch.

The suckers will grip your skin with a strange clinging touch which is quite disturbing, although harmless. In general you are not likely to be very much harmed by a European octopus, and certainly not poisoned.

Try to overcome any fear you may have, and get to know these handsome and beautiful relatives of the shellfish. They hide in small cave-like cavities and await the arrival of unsuspecting crabs. Then with a quick flurry of tentacles and a parachute-like spread of the body, it descends on its prey. I like octopuses for they are one of the very few marine creatures that spend some of their time *watching you*.

**Autumn** Sometime between mid-summer and early autumn there will be a sudden arrival of tiny, newly settled crabs. They drop out of the plankton as larvae (known as megalopa larvae) and change into a recognizable crab shape. At certain favourable times, the young crabs can be seen everywhere as their tiny transparent bodies gleam in the sun. By late autumn they will have grown into crabs.

With the passing of summer the young seabirds begin to come down to the shore and the air is filled with their mewling calls as they beg food from their parents. By this time most of the prawns will have left for deeper water and the sea-slug adults

An immature spiny spider crab showing its pincer claws not yet fully grown. You can sometimes find one in a low tide pool.

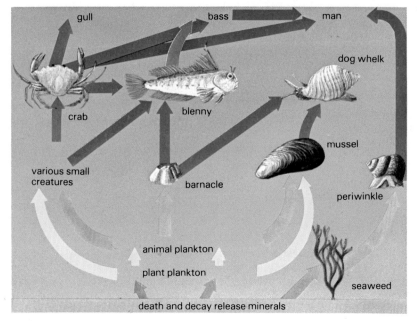

This food web shows some of the feeding connections to be found on the shore.

will have died, but a careful search will reveal many young shellfish and other young creatures.

Particularly common, although only appearing in certain parts of the shore, will be shoals of small mullet. On the beds of rock pools, tiny gobies and blennies up to 2 centimetres long can be seen darting about, but being almost transparent you will have to look carefully for them.

Under seaweed and rocks, mating crabs will be found, and this is simply preparation for the renewed release of life that will follow in the next spring.

The shore becomes quieter except

for an occasional screaming October gale that sends huge, bulldozing waves to tear at the seabed and cast thousands of shells on to the shore. As the waves crash down, they tear away many of the seaweeds which then get left on the strandline.

After a storm, the seabirds will move in, for amongst the stranded debris will be sea urchins, starfish, shore fishes, shell life of many kinds, crabs and worms.

This is all part of the seasonal cycle of life. It is part of the interlocking food webs, whereby one form of life depends upon another, and by means of which, all are able to survive as species.

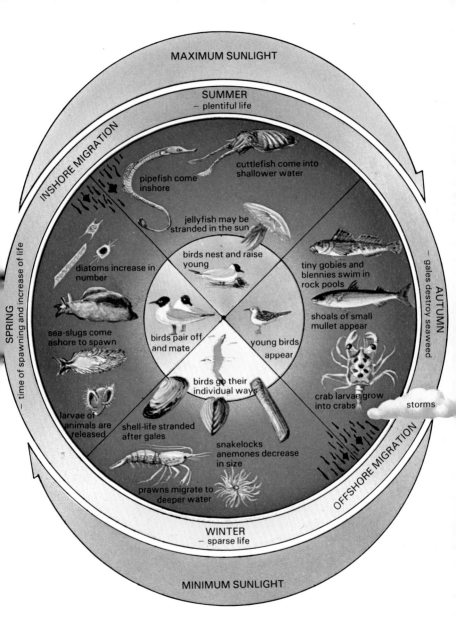

The cycle of life in the sea and on the shore continues from year to year.

Seabirds of many different kinds are to be seen along the seashore. By watching them over a period of time, it becomes easier to identify them. Their behaviour is fascinating to watch, as it changes with the seasons.

# Seabirds

## Gulls

If you walk along the shore you will soon come into contact with several different species of gull (Laridae). The herring gull (*Larus argentatus*) is dealt with in detail in the next chapter.

### Little gull
Until you get to know it well, you may confuse the black-headed with the little gull (*Larus minutus*), although this latter gull is very much smaller. Seen among black-headed gulls, it looks exactly like a miniature one. However, closer observation shows that although it has red legs, its bill is dark red in summer and blackish in winter.

In winter, the adult little gull has a similar head colouring to the black-headed gull, but in summer, it can be distinguished by a much blacker head which extends farther down the neck.

### Black-headed gull
A gull that is fairly easy to recognize is the black-headed gull (*Larus ridibundus*). It is a small gull, very light in flight, and in winter it has a small brownish spot on the face behind each eye. At first glance, and certainly at a distance, this spot appears as almost black.

By early February, this gull will be developing its summer plumage, as the dark spot spreads out and over the head, until the entire head is chocolate brown. This colour, plus the neat crimson bill and legs, make it a very handsome little gull.

It has a habit of perching in groups on promenade railings and sea walls, standing head to wind and waiting for someone to arrive with a bag of bread.

The black-headed gull is a delightful bird to watch in flight, for it is extremely agile, and some of its manoeuvres as it twists and turns are quite remarkable.

### Mediterranean gull
There is a third species of gull rather like the black-headed gull – the Mediterranean gull (*Larus melanocephalus*). In places where they overlap, you might find identification a little tricky. However, whereas the black-headed gull has black tips to the wings, the Mediterranean gull has pure white.

### Great black-backed gull
The largest gull you may encounter is the great black-backed gull (*Larus marinus*) which is instantly recognizable. It is very large and has a jet black back and pale pink legs. If you happen to hear one call, you will soon know it by its very deep and hoarse notes.

You will often see a pair walking

Kittiwakes come ashore in summer and form breeding colonies on cliff ledges. In the winter they spend their time at sea and are seldom seen inshore.

around a harbour when the tide is out, especially if fishing boats work there. They are on the lookout for pieces of fish and other offal found in such locations.

It's a fierce bird, and others keep well away from it. In the breeding season, it will swoop upon unguarded herring gull and other gull chicks, and even seize young rabbits and rats. There is little doubt that when it is hungry or has a growing family to feed, it will attack a variety of waders and other small birds, especially if they are wounded or less agile than their neighbours. I vividly remember one early morning watching a great black-backed gull that kept alighting on a buoy, after hovering over the sea. It did this several times, once even touching the sea surface, yet obviously it caught nothing. Then, during one of its flights from the buoy, it hovered for just a moment, and then plunged headlong into the sea.

A wild struggle ensued during which the gull seemed to struggle to haul something out of the water. With a particularly violent effort, it finally managed to rise from the surface with a very large cuttlefish hanging from its beak. At that same moment, the cuttlefish shot out a jet of sepia which blackened the breast of the gull. Undeterred, the gull flew off to some distant rocks where, no doubt, it breakfasted on fresh cuttlefish.

That incident typifies the sort of action you will see if you go about with your eyes wide open.

### Lesser black-backed gull

Much smaller is the lesser black-backed gull (*Larus fuscus*) which is about the same size as a herring gull. It is much more common than its larger relative, and with yellow legs, it is easy to identify. You will find it around harbours and river estuaries, and its general predatory habits are not unlike those of the great black-backed gull.

### The common gull

Contrary to its name, the common gull (*Larus canus*) is *not* common everywhere, and whilst it is similar in size to a herring gull, it has a greenish-yellow bill and legs, and its general appearance is much milder. Whilst the herring gull has a bold, searching, dominant look about it, the common gull is a meek, quiet and rather timid-looking bird. In winter its head is streaked grey.

### Iceland gull

If you are fortunate enough to see a large white and pale-grey gull (about the same size as a herring gull), you may well be watching an Iceland gull (*Larus glaucoides*). Especially during winter time, a few come south from the icy stretches of the Arctic, and will be seen in North Scandinavia and offshore islands of North Scotland. A few stragglers often stray as far as Spain and the Mediterranean.

### Kittiwake

One of the most delightful gulls to watch is the kittiwake (*Rissa tridactyla*) and the place to look for it is the cliff-bound coast, well away from disturbance.

In spring and summer, they gather together in colonies on narrow nesting ledges on the most inaccessible cliff faces. During this time of the year, the easiest way of identifying them is from their clear and very distinctive calls of 'Kitti-wake'. During the winter, they live far out at sea.

When I was learning the names of the different gulls, I found the best way was to watch them closely for some time, and so become familiar with their colours, general shape and even habits. Then, and *only then*, did I find a book useful. Once you know the features of a bird, you are able to look at pictures in a book and recognize it for sure, but first *watch* your birds.

---

## Terns

---

Birds of the same family as gulls, but much more elegant, graceful in flight, more slender in body and with forked tails, are the terns. A name frequently applied to them is 'sea swallows'.

Look out for the common tern (*Sterna hirundo*). It flies over the surface of the sea and then suddenly rises up to 30 or 40 metres, hovers for a few seconds and then plummets down into the sea. A splash follows as it hits the water, and then, it probably comes up with a sand-eel in its beak. With binoculars, you can sometimes see what one has caught, because common terns frequently go fishing close to the shore, and in open harbours at high tide.

## Auks

The Auks (Alcidae) are a group of seabirds whose colouring is black and white. When on shore, they stand upright rather like penguins, and when they move, they shuffle forwards in a rather ungainly manner. But in the water, they are fantastic swimmers, beautifully adapted to catch fish.

Unfortunately for the auks, their habit of swimming underwater often leads to their death. All too frequently, they come to the surface beneath an oil slick, or even swim into it, and so get their plumage covered in clinging, poisonous oil. In an attempt to clean themselves, they preen their feathers with their beak, and so swallow quantities of the stuff. This quickly burns and destroys their digestive tracts and throats, and leads inevitably to a painful and slow death.

### Guillemot
One of the commonest auks is the guillemot (*Uria aalge*). In the summer breeding season, they gather together in their breeding colonies on the side of a sheer, and usually very high, quite inaccessible cliff.

Here they crowd on to narrow ledges, often less than 20 centimetres wide, and lay their single eggs upon the bare rock.

When the young leave the nest, they spend quite a time in 'rafts' or small groups gathered together on the sea surface near to the base of the cliffs.

When hunting fish, the guillemot uses its wings to propel it through the water. Strangely enough, although this bird is so well adapted to life at sea, numbers of them are washed ashore every winter in a weak and wave-battered state. A few fortunate ones are rescued by naturalists, fed and strengthened, and then returned to the sea.

### Razorbill
Rather like the guillemot is the razorbill (*Alca torda*), but if you

Guillemots (pointed beaks) and razorbills (thick beaks) both catch their food underwater. Like other auks they fly in small flocks low above the water.

colony has nested for many years, the entire area of clifftop grass is honeycombed with their underground burrows, each one laboriously dug and scraped out by the puffin's feet. A single egg is laid and the young one reared, before the birds again depart for the open ocean, where they shed the bright bill covering and spend the winter fishing in the deep seas.

### Little auk

Tiniest of all is the little auk (*Alle alle*), barely as big as a blackbird. The best chance of seeing one of these birds is if one gets stranded during a gale. The odd single bird may be seen in winter anywhere from the Arctic, which is its true home, south to the Mediterranean.

## Other seabirds you may see

### Cormorant and shag

Two other diving birds must be mentioned: the cormorant (*Phalacrocorax carbo*) and the shag (*Phalacrocorax aristotelis*). I once asked a naturalist friend of mine who was a good birdwatcher, how he sorted out shags from cormorants when they were some distance away on the sea. He told me he called them either *cormorags* or *shagerants*. In other words, even an expert sometimes finds it difficult!

The shag however has no white on its thighs, although of course, this is a difference that only becomes

refer to the illustration, you will see that the bill is quite a different shape. When swimming, its tail sticks up. Much of its life is spent out in the Atlantic Ocean, far from land, and it is usually only seen inshore during the summer.

### Puffin

Perhaps most attractive of the auks is the puffin (*Fratercula arctica*). In the breeding season, its bill becomes highly coloured and striped with blue, yellow and bright red. It comes in from the open sea during March and April, and settles down to nest in rabbit burrows, or holes on turf-covered cliffsides, which the birds excavate themselves. Where a obvious when the bird is on land. The shag is also greenish-black, whereas the cormorant is glossy black, but it's not easy to see when the bird is some distance away. In summer, the shag has a crest on its head whereas the cormorant does not have one.

Both birds are excellent divers and catchers of fish, and if you happen to see one in an estuary, it will almost certainly be a cormorant, because the shag is strictly a seabird. So this is an instance where knowing the habitat of a bird is a most important guide to its identity.

Try timing the dives of cormorants and shags and other diving birds. Keep a record of your results, and you can then average them out for each species.

Another interesting observational exercise is to watch with binoculars and record the number of dives a bird takes before successfully catching a fish. You might be surprised to discover how hard a bird works to get its meals.

### Fulmar petrel

Often in a similar breeding area to the kittiwakes, you may see a fulmar petrel (*Fulmarus glacialis*). It has a gull-like appearance, but its wing tips are less pointed, and its neck much stouter.

It's a beautiful flier. Watch how it does a few wing beats and then glides, sometimes for several minutes, rising on thermals and updraughts and diving to gain speed – turning

every so often to 'patrol' the same familiar piece of cliff.

### Gannet

Gannets (*Sula bassana*) should be included in this list, although they are seldom seen close to the shore. Their very large size and black wing ends make them unmistakeable, and they dive like meteors into the sea to catch fish.

## Keeping a field notebook

Because there are so many very similar seabirds, it can be very difficult for a beginner to separate them. So, you must try to get to know your birds by steady and careful observation. Watch how they fly, check plumage colours and generally try to memorize distinctive features.

It is a great help to jot down a few observations on a sketch pad or notebook, using a basic bird shape to record your notes. The basic bird can be as simple as you like.

If you jot down details in this field notebook whilst you are looking at the bird, you can refer to a bird identification book when you return home. This is particularly important when you are trying to name birds that are rather alike, such as terns. Look carefully at the pictures in this book, then go out on to the shore, take some notes, watch and take more notes, and you will be surprised how quickly you learn to identify them all.

Gannets are fairly easy to recognize by their black wing ends and pale orange heads. However, before you get to know seabirds well, you will find it useful to record the features you see in a notebook (*inset*).

Here is a selection of seabirds that you may see.

# Gulls

Black-headed gull (summer)
length up to 41 cm

Little gull (summer)
length up to 28 cm

Mediterranean gull (summer)
length up to 38 cm

Great black-backed gull
length up to 69 cm

Lesser black-backed gull
length up to 53 cm

Common gull
length up to 41 cm

Iceland gull
length up to 56 cm

Sabine's gull (summer)
length up to 33 cm

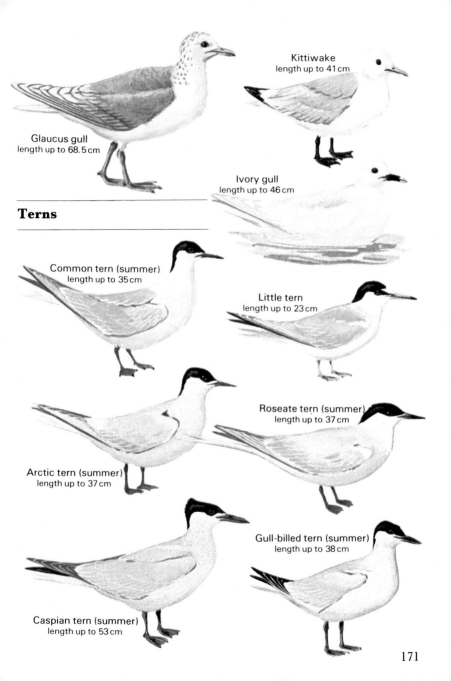

Glaucus gull
length up to 68.5 cm

Kittiwake
length up to 41 cm

Ivory gull
length up to 46 cm

# Terns

Common tern (summer)
length up to 35 cm

Little tern
length up to 23 cm

Roseate tern (summer)
length up to 37 cm

Arctic tern (summer)
length up to 37 cm

Gull-billed tern (summer)
length up to 38 cm

Caspian tern (summer)
length up to 53 cm

# Auks

Razorbill (summer)
length up to 41 cm

Guillemot (summer)
length up to 41 cm

Puffin (summer)
length up to 30.5 cm

Little auk (winter)
length up to 20 cm

Black guillemot (summer)
length up to 33 cm

Brunnich's guillemot (summer)
length up to 40 cm

# Other seabirds you may see

Cormorant
length up to 90 cm

Shag
length up to 76 cm

Fulmar
length up to 47 cm

Gannet
length up to 90 cm

Great shearwater
length up to 48 cm

Sooty shearwater
length up to 40.5 cm

Manx shearwater
length up to 35 cm

# The herring gull

The calls of herring gulls (*Larus argentatus*) and their flight patterns over the waves are familiar sights to every seashore naturalist. Yet, because of the familiarity with these birds, their fascinating behaviour is often overlooked. If you are keen on birdwatching, you will find few birds as interesting, and as easy to watch, as the herring gull.

In early spring herring gulls stand about in twos, quite close together. They are pairs, and it is now known that most herring gulls remain paired for life. However, they do not keep together during the entire winter, but, in some way that is not fully understood, they re-

Herring gulls gather wherever there is a possibility of food. Fishermen usually gut their catch on the way back to harbour and the gulls feed richly. Fish markets are also visited by the gulls. They often walk about on the decks of moored trawlers, picking up oddments left from the fishing trip.

unite with each other in late winter. From then on, they begin to go everywhere together, and that is when you will see pairs flying a few feet apart, or simply standing together on the beach.

As springtime moves on, the herring gulls return to their breeding grounds. According to the type of coastline, you will find these colonies either on cliff faces or sand dunes.

It is not easy to distinguish the male from the female, because there is no colour difference to help you, but there are some differences you can recognize. The male, for example, is much the larger of the two, and more upright in stance. His head is a little flatter, and generally he looks more powerful than his mate. You can, of course, only recognize the sexes when the two are together, because then you can compare one with the other.

## Courtship

The beginning of their courtship starts when the female bows low to the male, stretching her head forward and calling a low kee-ooo, kee-ooo, repeated many times. As she calls, she repeatedly raises her head quickly, and lowers it again. At first the male ignores her, but if she keeps it up for a while, he replies with a similar call and action. If you visit a colony in late spring, you will certainly see and hear this behaviour. Several times each day, the pair carry out this little ceremony, and it may be seen for 10 days or more.

Sometimes, the male reacts in a different way, and then his throat begins to swell and heave, until he regurgitates a large lump of partly digested fish which the female accepts. After a few more days, the pair will mate.

## Nestbuilding

When a colony is busy nestbuilding, you will see numbers of gulls flying with nest material held in their beaks. It is amusing to watch them, because you will see one fly off with a single short stem of bracken, whilst another must surely fly blind with a great tufted mass of dried grass blowing back over its head. The fun continues back at the nest for the site is usually very windy.

Often, the beakful of nesting material is dropped into position, only to be whipped away by the wind. The number of trips made by gulls before the nest is completed, is quite staggering.

Eventually, after much scraping and sitting in the growing nest, the final round shape begins to emerge, and the first egg is laid.

## Incubation and rearing the young

Herring gulls usually lay three eggs, and the pair share the business of incubating them. One goes off to feed whilst the other one sits in the nest. On sunny days, it is hot work, and then you will see the bird holding its beak half open, which is its way of cooling down.

On return to the nest, the other one of the pair utters a clarion call as it alights. This is a greeting. Shortly after this, they change over and the bird that has been incubating the eggs flies off to feed.

With the arrival of the chicks, the parents develop a very aggressive attitude towards you, should you venture too close. It is well worth your while listening for their alarm calls, but to hear them, you too will have to behave in a certain way. Generally, if you keep about 60 to 100 metres from the nearest nest, the gulls will take little notice of you, but if you begin to walk towards them, you will hear a distinct 'Ha-

Herring gulls courting. The female (*right*) walks around the male, begging and calling. This stimulates him to regurgitate food for her, and much later to mate.

ha, Ha-ha' call. At first, it will be quite soft, but as you draw closer, one or two gulls will utter the call more loudly. It is their alarm call, and they use it as a warning call to the entire colony.

If you continue to walk even closer, then you will hear a sudden screeching call, and the whole colony will begin to 'shout' at you, as the general panic spreads. Most of the gulls fly up screaming, and some will begin to swoop down on you.

When you first experience such an 'attack', it can be quite frightening for you are surrounded by screaming gulls, and every few seconds, one of them skims a few centimetres over your head, occasionally even touching you. But it's not the beak that touches you, only their feet.

The attacks will continue until you retreat, so never stay long in the defended territory. Try to do your watching from a distance and so cause as little disturbance to the birds as is possible.

*Above*: Three eggs is a normal clutch for a herring gull.

*Below*: The disruptive pattern and colour of the chick help it to conceal itself.

## Caring for the young

During the summer, you will be able to watch the parents feeding their chicks. When a chick wants food, it pecks at the red spot on its parent's beak. This 'begging' action causes the parent to regurgitate food that it has collected.

The chicks grow quickly, and in the crowded colony, there is always some bird trespassing on another's territory. The interesting thing about herring gulls is that they do not at first resort to fighting to settle the matter. Instead, occupant and intruder face one another and stretch their necks upwards, so that their whole body seems to grow larger. Slowly, they move towards each other, and stop. Then, suddenly,

Herring gull chicks peck the red spot on the parents' beaks when they want food.

one of them stabs at the grass, and begins to pull at it. Great effort is used, and the bird leans right back as it tries to tear out some grass – roots and all. During this action, the other one may watch or occasionally carry out similar activity. Whilst this is going on, wings are raised and each bird occasionally darts forward or leaps backwards.

All this behaviour is simply saying, 'This is my territory, keep out!' Generally, the intruder goes away, but if this warning fails, a fight starts and the two birds rush at one another. I have seen a herring gull seize another's wing and hold on for as long as four minutes. Throughout this time, they were lashing each other with their powerful wings. They ended the fight by toppling down the cliff, and only broke away from each other a few metres from the rocks below.

During the heat of the day, the chicks shelter under the leaves of a plant, or retreat into a shaded gulley, but as soon as one of their parents returns, they rush up to it, and start making their begging call. You cannot mistake this call, because it is thin and high pitched, quite unlike any other herring gull language.

From late summer into autumn, the action moves away from the colony, as the birds disperse to the shore. There, you will find the chicks still begging from their parents, and I have seen this happen as late as November.

Bathing is a daily routine throughout the year. Keeping plumage clean and in good order is most important for any bird to remain an efficient flier.

With the onset of winter, the herring gull 'families' break up. The chicks have begun to feed themselves, and the parent birds lead their separate lives until the next spring.

## Preening

Herring gulls, like any other animals, have some periods during which their behaviour consists simply of doing nothing at all. Mostly, this is at night, when they doze or sleep.

Often, after feeding, they will stand close to the nest site, keeping an eye on their chicks, and will then begin to preen. This is something you really must watch.

The beak is used to comb each feather into place, and to nibble gently at the long flight feathers,

with a little push here and a pull there. The beak is directed into the most astonishing positions, and I have taken photographs of a gull with its head doubled backwards over its back, pushed between its legs, or even twisted around under its tail. Occasionally, the bird uses its foot to gently scratch some part of the head.

Feathers are all-important to a bird, so they have to be kept clean, and in good order, and for this very reason, preening is a time consuming business.

## Cockling

This is an activity which is interesting to watch. The herring gull wades along at the edge of the sea, searching for any cockles that are not buried in the sand. If it finds one, it picks it up in its beak, and flies up to about 25 metres into the air. Then it lets the cockle fall and zooms down after it. On hitting the sand, the cockle shell usually breaks open, often shattering into several pieces, but sometimes, it does not break first time, so the gull has to try again.

The signs of this activity are to be seen on any beaches where cockles live. The white and broken pieces of shell will be found surrounded by the footprints of the herring gull. But you will not find any of the cockle itself – every piece is eaten and the shell pecked quite clean.

The time to look is on a spring ebbtide towards the time of low water. That's when the gulls are able to wade where the molluscs normally live. Why not collect some of these broken shells, mount them on card and include them in your seashore museum collection?

## Hints on equipment for watching

A pair of binoculars will be of great help, because they do bring the action so much closer. The variety on sale is enormous, but if you search carefully, and compare prices, you should be able to buy an inexpensive pair. If not, try to borrow a pair from a relative or friend.

If you are buying, then go to a shop and actually try them out. Make sure they are not too heavy,

because you will be holding them up to your eyes for quite long spells. A very big magnification makes it difficult to hold the image of the bird steady, and too small a magnification makes the bird so tiny that you see too little detail.

A hide is sometimes useful, especially if you want to get really close. However, it can be a problem too, because it is seldom possible to leave the hide unoccupied (vandals!) and so it has to be re-erected every time you go out. This disturbs the birds and gives them little time to become used to this new feature near their territory. Quite frankly, the best equipment for herring gull watching is your eyes, and a little patience.

Herring gulls use their wings to balance themselves when they are alighting.

# Seashells

Seashells are so common on every seashore that their varied shapes and different colours are often taken for granted. Their varied and amazing ways of life have already been covered. Some crawl slowly with snail-like speed, others swim swiftly through the sea. A few float and drift with the ocean currents, whilst many burrow deep into sand. Others anchor themselves to pier piles and some bore into rock and timber.

Fascinating animals make shells.

When you look at the 'dead' shells upon the beach, it is so easy to forget that once they were the home of a living creature, which actually made the shell itself. A shell is 98% calcium carbonate. Each shell consists of three layers of material, secreted by the animal. The inside layer is made up of a kind of calcium carbonate, which often looks like mother-of-pearl. Next to this, there is a thick middle layer of calcite, and finally, a thin outer layer of conchiolin which protects the rest of the shell against corrosive chemicals in the sea. This layer is frequently worn away in old, stranded shells.

As the shellfish grows, so it builds up and enlarges its shell around the open end, although there is, of course, a limit to the maximum size to which any particular species is able to grow.

This large and interesting group of soft bodied sea animals are known as molluscs.

Throughout the world, there are more than 100 000 different kinds, ranging from the giant squid with a body length of nearly 400 centimetres to tiny clams of less than 0·5 of a millimetre when fully grown.

One of the best ways of getting to know shells is to collect them. After rough seas, they are sometimes to be found on the shoreward side of rock faces, between boulders and in rock pools. As you begin to discover shells, you will find it becomes easier each time you search. You will develop an instinct for the best places.

## Collecting equipment

The most useful things to put shells in are plain plastic bags, although a few matchboxes or small plastic containers can be used for very tiny and delicate shells. These can be protected by a few pieces of crumpled tissue paper.

A plastic bucket is light to carry and will be useful on the wet shore. If you do fall, it will not shatter, and for that reason, never carry glass jars or any glass items on the shore. Very nasty cuts can result if you fall over whilst carrying them.

A haversack is favoured by many naturalists, but I find them a bit of a nuisance when bending about. In places where there are plenty of deep rock pools, a small net can be used to pick out shells too deep to wade in after.

## Sorting out the day's 'finds'

Many of the shells you collect will be perfectly clean, but others will have algal growths and mud on them.

I find the best thing is to treat them all the same. Pour the equivalent of half a cup of household bleach into a plastic bucket and add tap water to about half way up. Drop your shells into this solution and leave them for a day. As with the treatment of bones, be very careful. Bleach can hurt your eyes and certainly damage clothes. Ask an adult to help you.

Next day, pour the bleach solution down the drain and rinse your shells in several changes of clean tap water. They will then be ready to be spread out on sheets of newspaper and left to dry.

When thoroughly dry, they are ready to be sorted, so firstly pick out and throw away any damaged ones, or those with oil stains on them. Some of your shells will be covered with tubeworms and barnacles, and unless you like their appearance, these too should be rejected. Single valves of bivalves should also be cast out, along with badly worn shells and those with small holes in. You will then be left with some first quality shells fit for your collection.

## Storing the collection

Whilst professional naturalists may use multi-drawer, wooden cabinets, it is easy to improvise. Using simple containers in no way spoils the collection, and quite the best containers to use are shoe boxes.

Most shoe shops will be happy to let you have some of their surplus boot and shoe boxes, but in their original form, they are too deep to store shells. With a pair of scissors, reduce them in depth to about 5 centimetres, and use the lid of the box as a cover. The illustrations show you several ways of making cardboard cabinets.

Whilst shells can be placed directly on to the bottom of these boxes, it is best to put in a layer of cloth, tissue paper or – if you feel wealthy – cotton wool.

Ideally, only a single layer of shells should be kept in each box, but if you prefer, you can make cardboard trays to fit one on top of another. In this type of case, you keep your shoe box to its original size, and it will probably take three trays.

## Arranging a shell collection

There are many ways in which shells can be arranged as a collection.

You may fancy keeping them in families, in which instance you will use one or more boxes (or trays) for each family. A simple way is to arrange them as univalves and bivalves.

Interesting collections can be made by finding different sized limpets or periwinkles and arranging them in sequence. Many species of shells have a rich variety of colours, and of these, perhaps the flat periwinkle is the best. Their different colours look most attractive when laid out on one of your trays.

Another idea is to collect prey and predator. For instance, you could find as many different species as possible that have been attacked

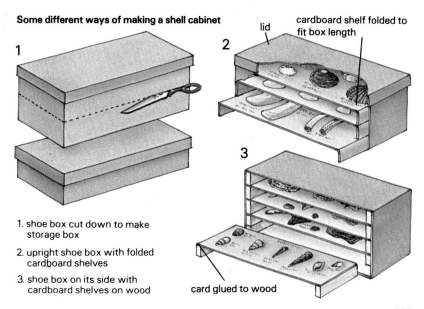

**Some different ways of making a shell cabinet**

1

2

lid

cardboard shelf folded to fit box length

3

card glued to wood

1. shoe box cut down to make storage box

2. upright shoe box with folded cardboard shelves

3. shoe box on its side with cardboard shelves on wood

by *Natica* and put them together. Dogwhelks and their prey can be treated in the same way.

Or how about collecting shells that have been broken open by sea-birds such as herring gulls? In estuaries, you will find mussel shells neatly 'drilled' by oystercatchers.

Shells that bore, or shells that burrow can be grouped together. You could separate them into herbivores and carnivores, or rocky shore and sandy shore and estuary species. There is also the habitat collection in which you could group together shells from the upper shore, those from the middle shore and those from the lower shore. There is no limit to the possibilities.

## Labelling

If the shells are to be stored in trays and are resting on some sort of soft base, you will have to cut out *small* pieces of card and write the names on these. These labels can be attached to the tray by a tiny blob of glue.

Shells mounted and glued to pieces of card should have their names written on the card itself. The date and place where they were collected can be added for future reference.

Each tray and each box of trays should be labelled according to its contents. You may think this is rather unnecessary, but as your collection grows, it will help you to find a specimen much more quickly.

## Identifying shells

If you look at the illustrations, you will see that the shells have been grouped together according to certain similar characteristics. The easiest way of getting to know such characteristics is to spend some time looking closely at some of the shells in your collection. At first, it is best to ignore colour, because some are so varied, and others simply bleached. So look at the *shape* of the shell.

For instance, is it a univalve or a bivalve? If it is a univalve is it rounded or pyramid shaped? Look at the underside opening: is it complete and rounded, or is there a groove cut into it? If it is a bivalve, are the valves roundish, oval, squarish or oblong? In other words, look closely and get to know it well. We have shown the more common shells here and suggested some books on page 216 which will help you with identification.

Whilst on the topic of naming, do not forget your local museum. Most museums have good named shell collections, and it will help you if you take yours along to compare them. Having named the shell in this way, put it in an old envelope and write the name on the outside, or do the same on a piece of paper and wrap the specimen in it. That way, you will still remember the name when you arrive home and return the shells to your collection.

Here is a selection of shells that you
may find.

Blue-rayed limpet
shell up to 1.5 cm long

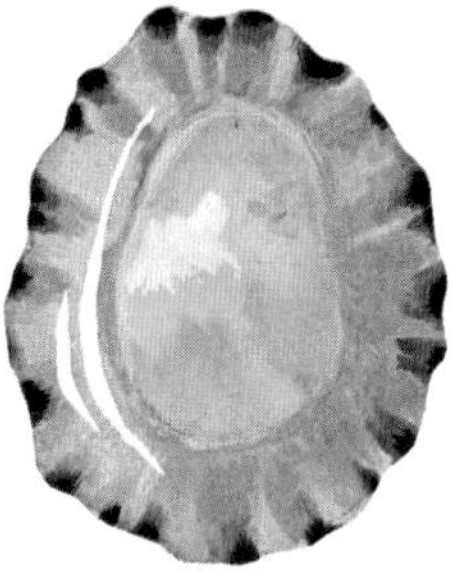

young

old

*Patella aspera*
shell up to 7 cm long

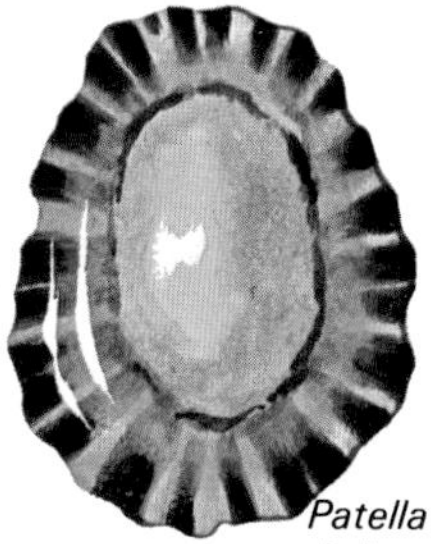

*Patella intermedia*
shell up to 4 cm long

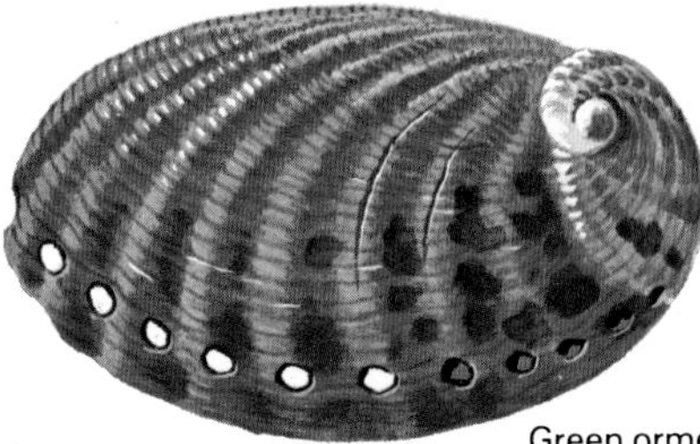

Green ormer
shell up to 8 cm long

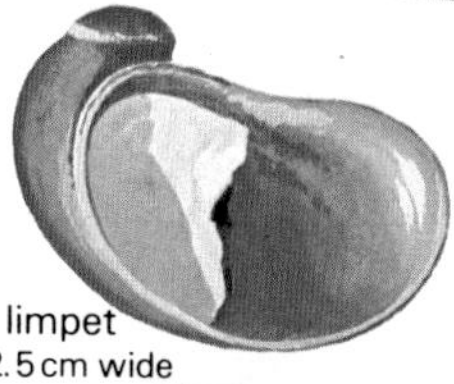

Tortoiseshell limpet
shell up to 2.5 cm long

Slipper limpet
shell up to 2.5 cm wide

Chinaman's hat
shell up to 0.7 cm high

Keyhole limpet
shell up to 4 cm long

Slipper limpets live in piles

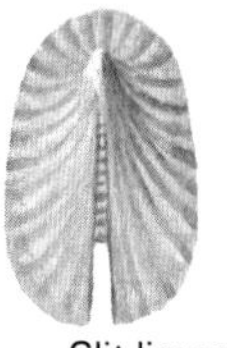

Slit limpet
shell up to 0.8 cm long

**Great top-shell**
shell up to 2 cm high

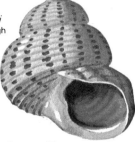

**Bonnet limpet**
shell up to 5 cm wide

**Variegated top-shell**
shell up to 2.3 cm high

*Gibbula adansoni*
shell up to 1.3 cm high

**Rough star-shell**
shell up to 5 cm high

*Monodonta turbinata*
shell up to 2.5 cm high

**Grooved top-shell**
shell up to 1 cm high

**Pheasant shell**
shell up to 0.8 cm high

*Clanculus corallinus*
shell up to 1 cm high

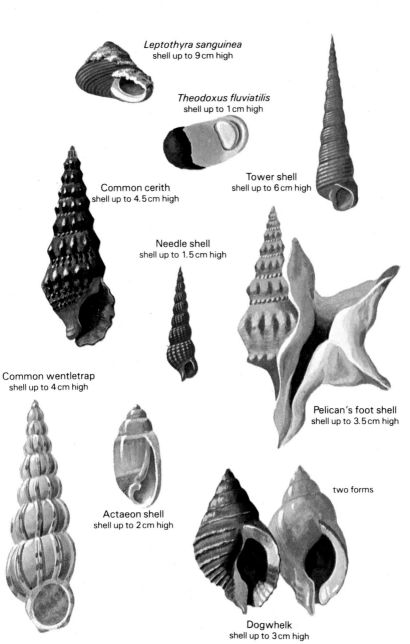

*Leptothyra sanguinea*
shell up to 9 cm high

*Theodoxus fluviatilis*
shell up to 1 cm high

Common cerith
shell up to 4.5 cm high

Tower shell
shell up to 6 cm high

Needle shell
shell up to 1.5 cm high

Common wentletrap
shell up to 4 cm high

Pelican's foot shell
shell up to 3.5 cm high

Actaeon shell
shell up to 2 cm high

two forms

Dogwhelk
shell up to 3 cm high

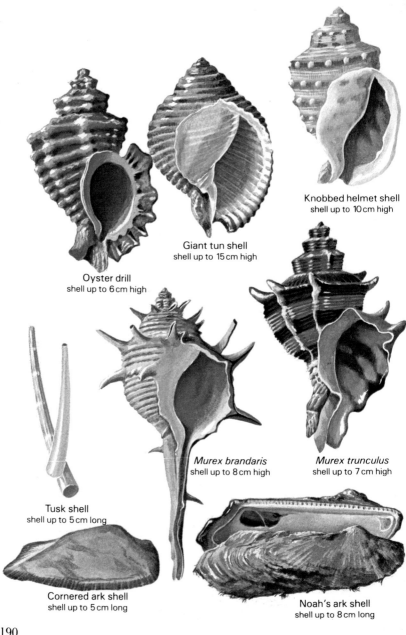

Oyster drill
shell up to 6 cm high

Giant tun shell
shell up to 15 cm high

Knobbed helmet shell
shell up to 10 cm high

Tusk shell
shell up to 5 cm long

*Murex brandaris*
shell up to 8 cm high

*Murex trunculus*
shell up to 7 cm high

Cornered ark shell
shell up to 5 cm long

Noah's ark shell
shell up to 8 cm long

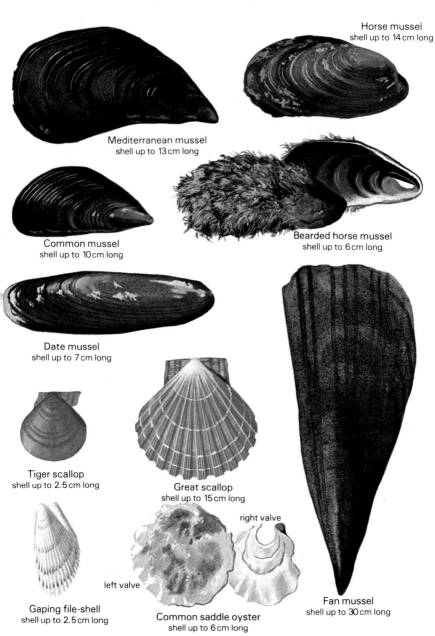

Horse mussel
shell up to 14 cm long

Mediterranean mussel
shell up to 13 cm long

Common mussel
shell up to 10 cm long

Bearded horse mussel
shell up to 6 cm long

Date mussel
shell up to 7 cm long

Tiger scallop
shell up to 2.5 cm long

Great scallop
shell up to 15 cm long

right valve

left valve

Gaping file-shell
shell up to 2.5 cm long

Common saddle oyster
shell up to 6 cm long

Fan mussel
shell up to 30 cm long

191

**Thick trough shell**
shell up to 4.5 cm long

**Rayed trough shell**
shell up to 5 cm long

*Dosinia lupinus*
shell up to 3.75 cm long

**Striped venus**
shell up to 4.5 cm long

**Warty venus**
shell up to 6.25 cm long

**Banded carpet shell**
shell up to 6 cm long

**Faroe sunset shell**
shell up to 5 cm long

**Banded venus**
shell up to 2.5 cm long

**Large sunset shell**
shell up to 6.25 cm long

**Oval venus**
shell up to 2 cm long

**Thin tellin**
shell up to 2 cm long

**Blunt tellin**
shell up to 6.25 cm long

**Flat tellin**
shell up to 6.5 cm long

**Peppery furrow shell**
shell up to 6.25 cm long

**Blunt gaper**
shell up to 7.5 cm long

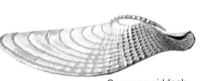

**Common piddock**
shell up to 15 cm long

**Flask shell**
shell up to 2.5 cm long

*Hiatella arctica*
shell up to 3.75 cm long

193

# Collecting methods

Collecting living specimens is something that should be carried out only occasionally and when it is, the greatest care should be taken of the livestock. Living specimens should only be collected when you need them for your aquarium and these should be returned later, alive, to the place of capture to make way for new creatures. Once caught, a good place to keep your specimens, temporarily, until you get home, is

It is surprising how many little animals live in the shallowest of sandy pools. Search slowly, and watch carefully. Then form a scoop with your hands to pick up any animals.

in a bucket full of seawater.

Much of the collecting done by the seashore naturalist depends upon some sort of net or fish trap. To be successful, it involves some knowledge of the habits of the animals. Whilst much of the equipment can be purchased from sports shops, a few items can be made at home.

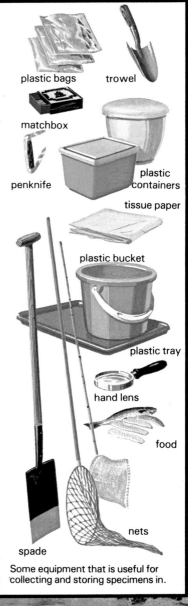

plastic bags

trowel

matchbox

penknife

plastic containers

tissue paper

plastic bucket

plastic tray

hand lens

food

nets

spade

Some equipment that is useful for collecting and storing specimens in.

## Prawn net

This is one of the most useful pieces of collecting equipment you can have. The best kinds of net are narrowly heart-shaped and you will be well advised to go for one of these rather than a circular one. The handle should be *very strong*, rather like a broomstick. Never buy thin wire-framed nets which bend over as soon as you start using them.

The diagram shows you how to make a prawn net from a broomstick, wire, cord and a piece of prawn netting. Fishing tackle shops often sell ready shaped pieces of prawn net which you can attach to your home-made frame.

### Method of use

Prawn nets are used on rocky shores to catch a variety of small fish like wrasse and of course, prawns of all sizes. If you enjoy paddling around in water, then you will enjoy prawning, but wear a pair of old shoes to protect your feet.

Look around near low tide until you find a stretch of water with plenty of seaweeds growing in it. Ideal places are large rock pools and lagoons with curtains of seaweed draped down into the water. This is because prawns and fish hide away in such places and may well be plentiful there.

Put the net gently into the water and slowly but steadily push it through the seaweed with one side of the net in contact with the rock face. Walk along for several metres, and then take a look to see what you have caught. If you can push the net into the narrow gullies and under rock ledges, then your chances of success are even greater. Depth does not seem to be too important. If the water is a metre or so deep, then do your first haul just below the surface and then return nearer the bottom.

## Shrimp net

Shrimps are found on sandy shores and you will require a special net to collect them in. I have yet to see a large shrimp net for sale, so in consequence always make my own. It's quite easy and the diagrams explain what you have to do. The actual size is up to you, but always have a *long, strong* handle.

### Method of use

The chapter on the sandy shore explains in detail how to use one of these nets and also shows you the variety of creatures you may catch.

## Drop net

If you have access to a stone jetty or concrete walled pier, a rocky platform with fairly deep water, deep rock pools and gullies, or seaweed covered harbour walls, you will be able to use a drop net.

**Making a prawn net**

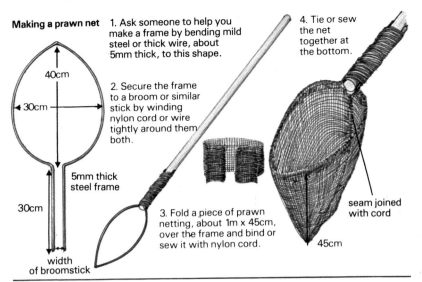

1. Ask someone to help you make a frame by bending mild steel or thick wire, about 5mm thick, to this shape.

40cm

30cm

5mm thick steel frame

30cm

width of broomstick

2. Secure the frame to a broom or similar stick by winding nylon cord or wire tightly around them both.

3. Fold a piece of prawn netting, about 1m x 45cm, over the frame and bind or sew it with nylon cord.

4. Tie or sew the net together at the bottom.

seam joined with cord

45cm

---

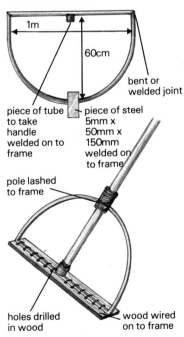

1m

60cm

bent or welded joint

piece of tube to take handle welded on to frame

piece of steel 5mm x 50mm x 150mm welded on to frame

pole lashed to frame

holes drilled in wood

wood wired on to frame

**Making a shrimp net**

1. Ask a metal worker or blacksmith to make this frame with mild steel. The steel can be flat or rounded but must be rigid. The piece of tube welded at the front and the steel at the top are to hold the handle.

2. Drill holes in a piece of wood, 12mm x 50mm x 1m, and wire it on to the base of the frame as shown. Lash a broom or similar stick to the frame with wire or nylon cord.

3. Fold and stitch a piece of netting, 3m x 6m, on to the frame. Start at the top by the handle and work right round. Trim the netting and sew it together at the end so that the net billows out behind.

It is simple to make, as you can see in the diagram. The outer frame of the net can be made from an old bicycle wheel rim or iron bar about 6 to 8 millimetres in diameter. Any metal workshop will weld it for you. Net, as in all this equipment, can be bought in some tackle or sport shops, but if you are near the sea, ask a fisherman if he will sell you a piece of small mesh netting.

The floats can be polystyrene fishing 'corks' found on the tide line or made from larger blocks of polystyrene. Wireless and refrigerator shops often have pieces to spare because their goods arrive packed in it, and it is usually thrown away.

You will probably have to buy the rope, and clothes line or cheap rope from an ironmonger's makes a good hauling line.

## Method of use

The idea behind a drop net is that it is baited with fish to attract crabs, prawns and small fish. So first of all, you need bait and this can be obtained – usually free – by asking your local fishmonger for flatfish skeletons. These are the pieces thrown away after a fish is filleted.

Tie your bait to the cross-string and lower the net as close as possible against the side of the fishing place, and continue to let it down until it rests on the seabed. Now you fasten the inshore end of the rope, and have a little patience as you wait for about 10 minutes for the specimens to arrive and start feeding.

To haul, pick up the rope and draw it in with a quick, steady pull. Whatever you do, be careful not to shake or jerk the rope as you pick it up. That would simply send your catch scurrying for cover, out of the net.

The net can be dropped into the same place several times, but if your catch is small, you should try another spot. The best time to try is after dark. Although you can use this net in the daytime you will catch far fewer specimens.

**Making and using a drop net**

1. Remove the spokes from an old bicycle wheel.

2. Take a piece of netting, about 45cm deep and long enough to go round the wheel.

## Fish traps

There are innumerable designs of fish traps from wicker baskets to iron cages, and the best thing to do is experiment with several types. By knowing your own seashore and the species that live there, you should be able to invent special traps. Try a few patterns of your own and see which works best.

The simple principle of a fish trap is that it is basically a cage with one or more specially designed entrances that are easy for a fish to enter through but difficult for it to escape through.

A good basis for a fish trap is an old, plastic bottle crate or something similar. Cover it with *very small mesh* wire netting, secured in place with thin wire. Entrance cones can be made from wire or thin bamboo.

Wooden traps are fine but these will require weighting with one or two suitably shaped stones.

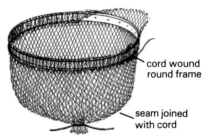

cord wound round frame

seam joined with cord

3. Fold the net over the wheel and bind or sew it with nylon cord. Tie or sew the bottom of the net together.

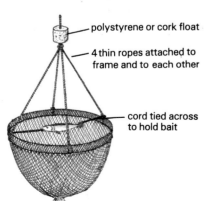

polystyrene or cork float

4 thin ropes attached to frame and to each other

cord tied across to hold bait

4. Attach ropes, floats and bait as shown.

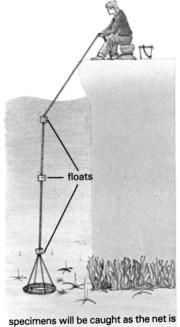

5. When using the net, lower it on to the seabed. You can attach the end of the rope to something while you wait.

floats

specimens will be caught as the net is hauled up.

The illustration on page 201 shows you how to make a fish trap.

**Method of use**

Fish traps should be placed at low tide in gullies, under rock ledges, in the corners of rock pools and similar 'fishy' places.

According to the species you are after, they can be baited or unbaited. Baited traps will catch crabs and prawns. Fish seem to enter unbaited traps simply out of curiosity, but they also tend to get out again more easily than other species.

Secure your trap by wedging it in place with a large rock, or even tie it in place if there is anywhere to fix a rope or wire. Leave it there until the next low tide before returning, hopefully, to collect your catch.

If you have a boat, traps can be lowered in deeper water with a rope secured to a float on the surface, to mark their position.

There is really no limit to the possibilities, and it's good fun trying your ideas out, especially when you catch your first wrasse or scorpion fish in a trap designed and made by yourself.

# Drag net

This is a specialized net that can be used only in a few limited locations. Ideally it should be dragged along the *flat* cement walls of harbours or piers, since any real roughness or projection in the wall prevents its use. Snags such as mooring chains, mooring eyelets and similar obstructions make the job even more difficult. However, if you know a place where a net can be used, you will be richly rewarded with specimens of all kinds. I know one such concrete jetty where I can haul the net for over 100 metres, free of snagging problems. A typical catch in that place would be ten prawns, three small wrasse, two spider crabs, two velvet swimming crabs, four green shore crabs, a pipefish, a sea stickleback, a small pollack (in season) and, with a little luck, even a feather star.

**Method of use**

Simply lower the net into the water and start walking, paying out the hauling rope until it's nearly all gone. Take the strain and drag the net to the end of the place, before hauling it out. It helps if you fill your buckets with water and take them forward to the hauling point *before* you start fishing. It's difficult to drag a net with one hand and carry two water filled buckets in the other!

# Small trawls and dredges

These are used from boats, and their design depends upon the power of the motor, nature of the seabed and – not least – your own strength. If you own a boat and want to try a

## Making a fish trap

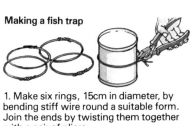

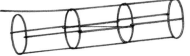

1. Make six rings, 15cm in diameter, by bending stiff wire round a suitable form. Join the ends by twisting them together with a pair of pliers.

2. Join four rings together by twisting four 70cm lengths of wire through them so that they are at equal distances from one another.

4. Make two more wire rings 4cm in diameter and join each, with netting, to one of the remaining 15cm wire rings to form cones. Make a paper guide as shown to cut the two cones of netting from.

3. Wrap some small-mesh wire netting or prawn netting around the frame. Join the seam by twisting the ends together (wire netting) or by sewing with cord (prawn netting).

30cm

30cm

6cm

30cm diameter

cone tied with string so that it can be removed and replaced

cone fixed securely in place

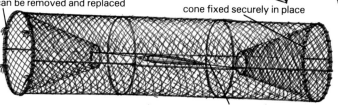

5. Fix the cones in place in the frame and bait the net as shown.

wire fixed across to hold bait

## Using a drag net

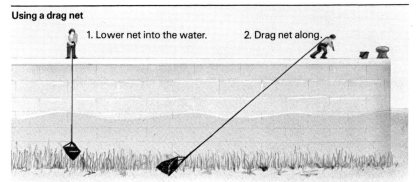

1. Lower net into the water.

2. Drag net along.

trawl or dredge, you will be well advised to have a chat with a local fisherman. Most of them enjoy helping young people make a net, and their advice is always based on wide, local experience.

## Crab and lobster pots

These can be copied from pots on your local harbour, or you may be able to buy an old one from a professional crabber. Again, you will need a boat, but the use of these pots barely comes within the work of a seashore naturalist. Nevertheless, if you want to know how to use them, you should ask a fisherman to help you.

## Maintenance

All collecting gear should be kept in very good condition. Each new

There are several kinds of nets and pots used for fishing. Each sort is suitable for different species. Here are some you may see and you can copy these if you want to try to make your own for collecting different specimens. You will need a boat if you are going to use a trawl net.

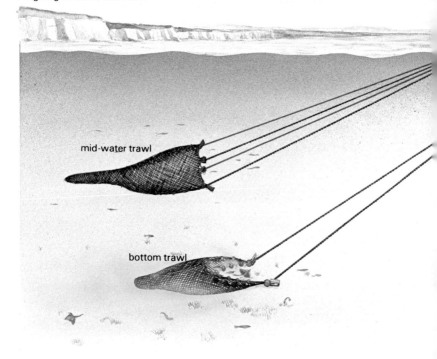

mid-water trawl

bottom trawl

season you should test your nets for strength, and hauling ropes, harness, wires and so on should be looked at most carefully. There is nothing as disappointing as losing a net because a rope breaks, or losing a specimen because the net had a hole in it.

Rust is your enemy. Chafing is a constant source of trouble. Untidy and damp storage weakens everything.

One of the most exciting things you can do is go out with good equipment you have made yourself. As you get near the water, you begin to think of all those rare and interesting creatures you are going to catch. You start fishing, using all your skills and knowledge and then the great moment comes when you look into your net, and see for the first time, a new capture. It's a terrific feeling and one that you enjoy every time you go to the seashore.

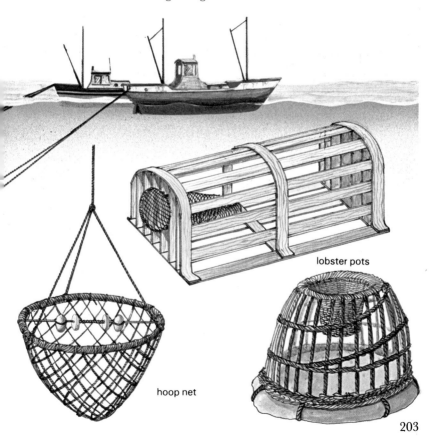

lobster pots

hoop net

# Marine aquariums

A marine aquarium is easy to set up, and, with a little care, it is easy to maintain. It's a marvellous way of observing many of the creatures you find on the shore, because you can watch them so closely. Many shore animals quickly settle down in the small space provided and lead their normal lives.

## Air pumps

Firstly, you will need an air pump with a length of plastic tubing and an air diffuser stone. The pump works on electricity. It sends air under pressure along the tube, and this air is then forced out through the diffuser stone, and rises as a stream of tiny bubbles. This flow of air keeps the water aerated and moving – two requirements of many sea creatures. A plastic or metal tap (or stop-cock) fixed to the air line controls the rate of flow of the air.

Air pumps vary in price according to the amount of air they produce, but for a single small marine aquarium, the smallest pump is ideal.

## Filters

If you can afford it, a biological sub-sand filter helps to keep your aquarium in good condition. Such a filter consists of a small network of plastic tubes with tiny holes in them connected to the airline from your pump. These tubes should be covered by 2·5 centimetres of sand in the bottom of the aquarium tank. When air slowly enters the tube system, it draws water down through the sand, which thus filters it, and then passes the cleaned water back into the aquarium.

Biological or sub-sand filters can be bought at all pet shops. If you get one, you will need a T junction to fix its airline to your existing supply from the pump, and another tap to control the flow.

An alternative kind of filter can be attached to the side of the aquarium. This sort is filled with glasswool which acts as a filter. The water is syphoned from the aquarium into the filter then through the wool. It is returned to the aquarium via an airlift tube. In my experience, the sub-sand filter is by far the most efficient.

If you are prepared to save up a lot of money, you might prefer to buy an Eheim seawater filter and pump. This consists of a cylinder in which glasswool and charcoal are inserted. There is a pump on the top which draws water out of the aquarium, forces it through the filter medium and returns it to the tank. The pump in this model does not use air, but physically moves the water by means of plastic vanes.

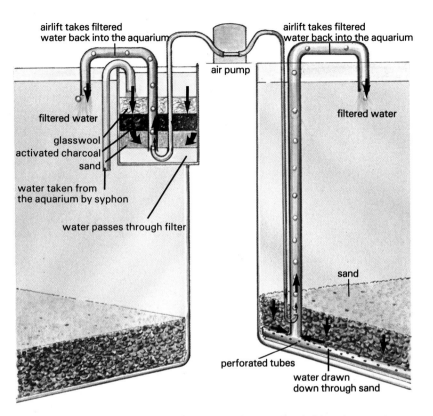

airlift takes filtered
water back into the aquarium

airlift takes filtered
water back into the aquarium

air pump

filtered water

filtered water

glasswool

activated charcoal

sand

water taken from
the aquarium by syphon

water passes through filter

sand

perforated tubes

water drawn
down through sand

Two airlift filters. *Left*: Water is drawn through a filter medium held on the aquarium.
*Right*: Airlift draws water through a sub-sand biological filter at the bottom of the
aquarium.

To start with, I would recommend you use a simple air pump and sub-sand filter. You can always try other ideas as you gain in experience.

## Aquariums

Since seawater is a complex mixture of chemicals, it does react with many different kinds of metals. The result can cause all sorts of unpleasant waste products and poisons, so avoid metals coming into contact with the seawater. Glass and plastic are perfectly trouble free.

You will have to decide how much you can spend and what size aquarium you have space for. Pet shops sell aquariums of many different sizes but a good size to begin with is about 450 millimetres long ×

250 millimetres wide × 250 millimetres deep. Choose one with plastic edging, and avoid angle iron, as this rusts very quickly. Rust will not hurt your livestock, but it looks very unsightly and eventually leads to leaks.

An alternative is to make your own. Five pieces of glass, cut to size, are glued together with one of the glazing substances in tubes, sold by petshops. Aquaseal will glue glass together very well.

Glass surfaces should be perfectly clean, and the base laid on a flat surface. Give one edge of one of the sheets forming the sides a thick coating of the sealing glue. Place this sheet in position on the base and hold it upright with a pile of books or any object to prevent the sheet falling out of the vertical. Use a set square to make sure it is vertical.

In turn, treat the other sheets in the same way. Remember to draw a damp cloth up the joined edges. This will flatten the bead of glue and so increase the strength of the joint. Reference to the diagrams will help you to see how the aquarium is assembled.

The great advantage of making your own aquarium is that you can make it exactly the right size for your own needs.

## Rock pool aquariums

Plastic basins, large china bowls, or shallow glass aquariums are fine for using as small rock pools. Even a

**Making an aquarium**

1. Use five sheets of glass − four of the same height in pairs of the same width, and one sheet for the base to be 3cm wider all round.

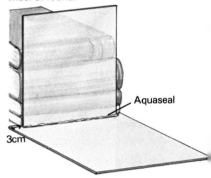

Aquaseal

3cm

2. Glue along the bottom edge of one side piece of glass and lower into position on the base.

3. Use a pile of books to hold the first side of the aquarium in position

sheet of polythene arranged so as to line a small box will make a temporary home for your livestock.

However, prawns and small fish tend to leap out when frightened by your sudden appearance above them. Crabs crawl out too, so the container should have a cover.

## Setting up your aquarium

Try to arrange it so that it is away from direct sunlight, and in as cool a place as possible. Do not use artificial light. After all, most of the creatures shun light and favour the shaded parts of the shore.

Place your aquarium on a stand or table that is solid and firm. Water is very heavy − 1 litre weighs approximately 1 kilogram.

4. Glue the second side of glass and lower it into position as shown. Place a book on top to hold the two pieces together.

6. Glue along the remaining vertical edges of the second and third sides of the aquarium and along the bottom edge of the fourth side. Lower the fourth side carefully into position.

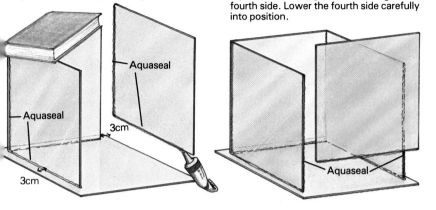

Aquaseal

3cm

Aquaseal

3cm

Aquaseal

5. Glue and position the third side in the same way.

**NB** When joining all the edges, remember to rub a dampened cloth along the join to spread the glue evenly.

## Seawater

If you live within a reasonable distance of the coast, then seawater should be collected from your nearest seashore. Go to a place well away from any freshwater outfall, sewage or other pollution, and collect it only when the sea is absolutely clear – never after a gale. If you have ever carried water any distance, you will know some of the difficulties. It's very heavy, it has a habit of slopping over the edges of any container, and if you are carrying it by car, half of it finishes up on the floor. To save all this trouble, line your container with a plastic bag, pour the water inside and tie the top to

prevent spillage. Bin liner bags are ideal for this purpose, but many shops sell assorted sized plastic bags, and you should find no problem in getting one.

Buckets make convenient containers and strong cardboard boxes can be used, providing the bag inside is fairly strong. If you buy 500 gauge heavy plastic bags, you will not need any container. Simply carry your bag of water home.

Artificial seawater is easily obtained from pet shops, but it is rather expensive. Full instructions for mixing it will be found on the packet, and there is no doubt that, for the inland aquarist, it provides a simple answer to the water supply problem.

## Sand

Every marine aquarium is better with 3 centimetres of sand on the bottom. Choose a coarse sand rather than a fine grained one, as the former has less tendency to create pollution pockets.

You can use most sands – either marine or river. Seashore sands are best, but many local authorities have bylaws against the collection of sand from their beaches. It is a good idea to check first.

Builders' sand is suitable too, but whenever you introduce sand to your tank, wash it thoroughly first. Stir half a bucket of sand vigorously under running tap water and then allow it to settle. Pour the dirty water off, and repeat this several times until no more dirt is washed out.

The fact that your sand is now soaked in freshwater does not matter. Put it into the aquarium and remember to put a filter in place *before* adding water.

## Creating the habitat

Rockwork is essential, but its type and layout will depend upon the sort of creatures you intend to keep. Rocks and stones are best taken from the natural environment of your collected specimens.

Anemones and limpets are examples of species that require rockwork on which to attach themselves. Crabs like to have the shelter of a small rock cave in which to hide away. Small wrasse seem to enjoy a rocky environment to swim around in. Brittlestars and starfish drape themselves over rocks.

In a small aquarium, the average rock should be about the size of a tennis ball or orange, and if you search carefully, you will be able to find some colourful or beautifully shaped pieces which will add much to the general appearance of your aquarium. If you periodically change the rocks, you will be able to have an ever-changing environment which makes the aquarium more interesting.

You can buy miniature shipwrecks, divers and plastic sharks, but these do nothing to heighten the beauty of the aquarium. What you should aim for is a good reproduction of a small rock pool.

Many rocks on the seashore will have a growth of seaweed on them, but although they may look attractive, you will be inviting problems. Seaweed needs very precise conditions in which to grow, and few aquarists can supply these. The trouble is caused when the seaweed dies and poisons the water – and it is not easy to tell when this is beginning.

## Livestock

A little knowledge of the habits of

Some animals that you can watch in a small aquarium.

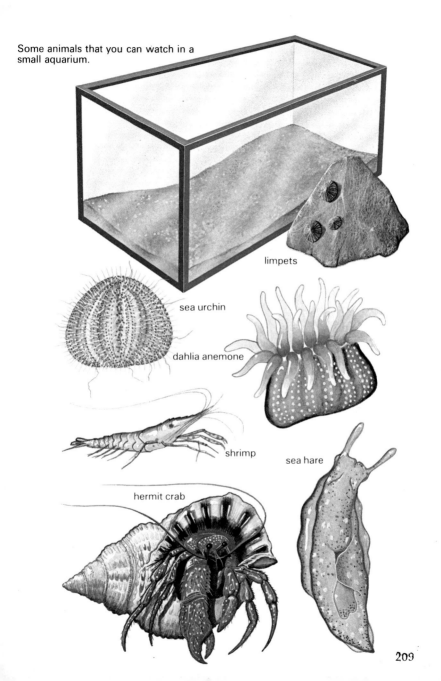

limpets

sea urchin

dahlia anemone

shrimp

sea hare

hermit crab

marine life will help considerably when you need to decide what to keep in an aquarium.

You may have discovered a great deal for yourself by actual observation on the shore, but this knowledge is best supplemented by reading. Most good reference books contain plenty of useful information on animals' behaviour and this helps to sort out your problems.

Two main problems exist. The first is which kinds of animals to keep, and the second is how many to keep in your particular aquarium. Whilst it may be interesting to watch a fish catch and eat a prawn, it is not much fun if too many of your specimens begin to feed on each other. So you have to think about prey and predator, and also the relative sizes of what you intend to keep.

Here is a typical mixed collection: 3 prawns (*Leander squilla*) but not larger than 40 millimetres each; 1 green shore crab (*Carcinus maenas*) about 50 millimetres across its back; 3 beadlet anemones (*Actinia equina*); 1 snakelocks anemone (*Anemonia sulcata*); 1 common starfish (*Asterias rubens*) 100 millimetres maximum; 2 blennies of any species and 1 wrasse of any species.

Another idea is to have a single species collection. For instance, an aquarium filled with many different anemones is a delightful sight and can continually be added to as you find new species.

It takes a while for newly caught specimens to settle down. Some take up territory. Crabs, for example, will soon find a favourite hide-away, and small fish will begin to swim in one particular part of the aquarium.

Perhaps the best way of all to decide which creatures get along together, is to try them in your aquarium – and *watch* them. You will soon see signs of aggression, and you can then return the offender to the seashore.

## How and when to feed the livestock

Details of particular foods are included in the notes on species which follows, but one golden rule applies: feed little rather than too much. Twice a week is enough, and all uneaten food left on the aquarium floor should be removed within an hour after feeding. Otherwise, it decays and poisons the water.

If you are using fish as food, avoid any oily fish such as herring and mackerel, as the oil from their flesh dirties the water.

### Sea-squirts
Sea-squirts feed by filtering seawater, so if you keep these, you will need to mash up a pea-sized piece of fish and release it near to the sea-squirts. If you watch closely you may see them sucking some of the pieces in. Keep the water stirred, so that this food passes by them – they cannot 'bend down' to feed.

Feeding an anemone.

### Anemones
Cut some fresh fish into pieces about the size of the end joint of your little finger. Place one or two pieces directly amongst the tentacles with a pair of tweezers. Feed the anemones twice a week.

### Brittlestars
These little animals catch food on their long, fragile arms. Offer them tiny match-head sized pieces of fresh fish, by placing them on the tips of their arms with a pair of tweezers. You will be able to watch how they pass the food down from tube foot to tube foot, all the way to the mouth which is at the central meeting place of the arms.

### Sea urchins
Some species rasp algae from rock surfaces whilst others eat pieces of fish. Give them a stone that has a plentiful growth of moss-like algae on it. If they don't eat the algae, give them pea-sized pieces of fresh fish. They eat this if you place it in contact with the base of the animals.

### Sea cucumbers
These are strange and fascinating creatures which when frightened or disturbed, throw out long sticky threads, or even eject their entire internal organs (which they grow again). Offer them pieces of fish.

### Shrimps and prawns
The food requirements of these animals are very simple. Give them small pieces of fish three times a week.

### Lobsters and crayfish
You will be fortunate indeed if you find a small specimen of these, because few people have ever done so. However, if you do find one, feed it on pieces of fish.

### Porcelain crabs
These delightful little crabs feed on plankton which they draw towards their mouths by fanning their mouthparts to set up a flow of water. Feed them in the same way as sea squirts.

### Crabs
In general, crabs are scavangers and will eagerly eat any dead matter like molluscs, fish and even dead crabs. Feed them on pieces of fish and you will find that, like lobsters, they have large appetites.

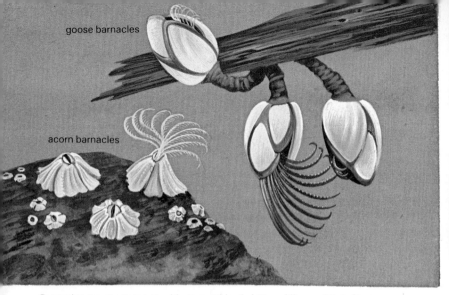

goose barnacles

acorn barnacles

Barnacles are crustaceans with an outside skeleton of limey plates. Some are very common on the shore, but goose barnacles drift around on floating objects.

## Barnacles

If you watch closely, you will see these creatures 'fishing' with their net-like feet. When they are busy 'fishing' spread a little mashed up fish into the water and keep it circulating near them so that they can collect it.

## Starfish

If you keep starfish, only have them up to 15 centimetres across. Offer them pieces of fish about the thickness of a pencil and 3 centimetres long. Place the fish on the underside of one of their arms and they will then draw it along to their mouths. It is sufficient to feed starfish once a week. Occasionally you can offer starfish a mussel, cockle or some other bivalve shellfish and then you will be able to see how it feeds more naturally.

## Shell-life

Shell-life is so varied in its food requirements and each species is so specialized that you will have to read up the needs of your particular specimens.

## Sea-slugs

The colours and shapes of these animals are quite extraordinary and most are highly specialized feeders. The common grey sea-slug attacks and eats snakelock anemones and the sea-lemon enjoys sponges such as the breadcrumb sponge. If you collect others and wish to keep them, you will have to refer to specialist books on the subject.

## Squids and cuttlefish

The little cuttlefish are good aquarium animals, and they are easy to feed. Offer them either tiny crabs, or small shrimps, but any food offered must be alive. Do not keep them with fish or crabs because they will eat them.

## Worms

Vast numbers of worms of all kinds are common on the shore and you may well want to keep some. Ragworms can be fed on pieces of fish whilst sand mason worms should be offered mashed fish presented at the open end of their tubes. The tube worms are very beautiful and can be fed on mashed fish in very small quantities. Unfortunately, most worms are eaten by a wide range of sea creatures, so you will have to keep them in an aquarium by themselves.

## Fish

The dazzling array of fishes around European coasts numbers many hundreds. Many of the smaller species, up to 150 millimetres, settle down in the limited space offered by an aquarium and make most attractive inhabitants.

Most popular are probably the wrasse family and they will eat prawns and crabs. They are particularly attractive because they swim in midwinter and so fill up that otherwise vacant space.

Blennies quickly become tame and will take pieces of fish from your hand. If you keep these little fish, always include a rock which extends above the surface of the water with a gentle slope. Some species like to come out of water after dark and you will almost certainly find them clustered together.

Young mullet will sometimes be found in river estuaries, harbours and occasionally in rock pools. In aquariums they swim between midwater and the surface. Keep about six of them, each about 5 to 7 centimetres long. They can be fed on tiny pieces of fresh fish and they quickly learn to come to a particular place for food.

The sea perches which include the bass (*Dicentrarchus labrax*) if caught when small enough, adapt well to aquarium conditions. They grow fast, but like most fish, their size will be limited in aquarium conditions. Bass enjoy live food especially small crabs, shrimps and prawns.

During your explorations of the seashore, you will find all kinds of fish and no doubt take many of them home. Confine your collecting to the small specimens for they will thrive, especially if you do a little research into their natural foods in the sea and supply them with what they need.

Of all the animals you are likely to keep, fish are most sensitive to lack of oxygen in the water, so if you keep fish, you must be sure that they have a constant supply of air.

# Glossary

**Adaptation** Any feature of a living animal or plant which improves its chance of survival in the environment (qv) it inhabits.

**Algae** Simple photosynthetic plants including seaweeds.

**Amphipoda** Order of Crustacea (qv) including shrimps, sandhoppers.

**Annual** A plant that completes its life cycle from seed to death in a single season.

**Antenna** A jointed whip-like organ (paired) on the head of insects, crabs and other animals, used as a sense organ for touch and smell and sometimes for swimming.

**Bivalve** An animal with a shell in two parts hinged together (eg cockle, scallop).

**Camouflage** Means by which an animal is made indistinguishable from its background.

**Carnivore** A flesh eater

**Chlorophyll** The green pigment found in leaves and plants. It is located in chloroplasts and is important to the process of photosynthesis (qv).

**Classification** The system of classing organisms in a hierarchical series of groups. The smallest group is the *species* which are grouped together in a *genus*. *Genera* are grouped together in *families* which in turn are grouped into *orders*, *orders* into *classes*, *classes* into *phyla* (animals) or *divisions* (plants), *phyla* or *divisions* into *kingdoms*. *Kingdom* is the highest rank.

**Conservation** The art of understanding and caring for the world we live in.

**Crustacea** A class of animals including shrimps, crabs.

**Deposit feeder** An animal that eats items that settle on the seabed around it.

**Distribution** The way in which plants and animals are spread around an area.

**Embryo** The stage in the development of an animal before birth or hatching from an egg.

**Environment** A term used to describe the conditions in which a living thing lives (eg light, moisture, dryness, temperature).

**Habitat** The place inhabited by a particular living thing.

**Herbivore** A plant eater.

**Hermaphrodite** A plant or animal having male and female parts.

**Holdfast** The base part of a seaweed, which anchors it to the ground.

**Larva** The pre-adult form in which some animals hatch from the egg.

**Migration** The movement or journey of a living thing from one place to another.

**Mollusca** A phylum of soft-bodied animals, often with a hard shell, including mussels, snails, octopuses.

**Organism** Any form of animal or plant life.

**Parasite** An animal or plant that lives upon another to obtain its food.

**Perennial** A plant that continues to grow year after year.

**Photosynthesis** The process by which green plants turn the mixture of carbon dioxide and water into sugar using energy from sunlight absorbed by chlorophyll (qv).

**Plankton** Drifting animal and plant life in the sea and freshwater.

**Pollution** Any form of object that causes physical or visual damage to our living world and its plant and animal inhabitants.

**Predator** An animal that feeds on other animals not including parasites (qv).

**Regeneration** The regrowth of part of an animal or plant that has been removed.

**Regurgitation** The act of bringing back through the mouth food that has been swallowed.

**Secretion** A substance given off by part of an animal or plant.

**Sedentary** An animal that remains in one place attached to a fixed object.

**Suspension feeder** An animal that takes in food that is floating in the water which surrounds it.

**Univalve** An animal with a shell in a single piece (eg limpet, snail).

An example of pollution on the shore.

# Further reading

If you are interested in reading more books about the seashore, here is a short list of suggested books that will help you decide where to start your collection. You may be interested in the general seashore or a certain aspect of it.

## General books

*The Sea Shore:* C M Yonge (Collins New Naturalist Series). This book is very easy to read and contains many fascinating facts about seashore life.

*The Hamlyn Guide to the Seashore and Shallow Seas of Britain and Europe:* A C Campbell (Hamlyn). This is a beautifully illustrated book that will help you to identify specimens.

*Collins Pocket Guide to the Sea Shore:* John Barrett & C M Yonge (Collins).
This is one of the best books for general identification. It has excellent illustrations and excellent keys.

*Marine Life:* DeHaas & F Knorr (Burke Young Specialist Look at Series).

*The Beach:* Leslie Jackman (Evans Bros).

*Exploring the Seashore:* Leslie Jackman (Evans Bros).

## Books about shell-life

*British Shells:* Nora McMillan (Warne Wayside and Woodland Series).

*Life of Animals with Shells:* Whybrow (Macdonald Education Introduction to Nature Series).

## Books about seaweeds

*Seaweeds of the British Isles:* Peter Dixon and Linda Irvine (British Museum).

*Seaweeds of the seashore:* Angel (Jarrold).

## Books about fish

*Key to the Fishes of Northern Europe:* Alwyne Wheeler (Warne).

## Books about the coast

*The Sea Coast:* J A Steers (Collins New Naturalist Series).

*Coasts and Estuaries:* Richard Barnes (Hodder and Stoughton).

## Books about plankton

*The Open Sea – The World of Plankton:* Alister Hardy (Collins New Naturalist Series).

## Books about birds

*The Young Birdwatcher:* Nicholas Hammond (Hamlyn).

*The Hamlyn Guide to Birds of Britain and Europe:* Bertel Bruun and Arthur Singer (Hamlyn).

## General reading

Some of the most interesting books were written by Philip Henry Gosse. He was a Victorian naturalist who described his discoveries on the seashore. The books are now out of print, but libraries have them and you can obtain them through the County Library Service. His books include: *The Aquarium*; *A year at the Shore*; *A Naturalist's rambles on the Devonshire Coast*; *Tenby: A Seaside Holiday*.

There are lots of other books that have been written about life on the seashore. New books are always being published whilst other, older ones go out of print. If you ask at your local library, the librarians will be pleased to help you. Simply tell them that you are looking for books on the seashore, or whatever aspect you are interested in, and they will either tell you where to look for them, or they will get them for you.

Most large cities and towns have specialized libraries in the museums and in 'learned societies' such as natural history societies. For a small fee, you can sometimes obtain copies of special articles published in scientific journals.

Eggs of the common cuttlefish in eel grass, looking like bunches of black grapes.

# Index

223